"Seek My Face"

Prayer as Personal Relationship in Scripture

William A. Barry, S.J.

Paulist Press
New York and Mahwah, N.J.

Imprimi Potest

Very Rev. Robert E. Manning, S.J., Provincial Society of Jesus of New England

All scripture quotations, except those listed below, are from the *Holy Bible, New International Version.* Copyright © 1973, 1978, 1984 by International Bible Society. Used by permission of Zondervan Bible publishers.

Psalms are from *Psalms Anew In Inclusive Language.* Copyright © 1986 by Saint Mary's Press.

The translation of the Magnificat in Chapter XI is from *The Jerusalem Bible.* Copyright © 1966, 1967, 1968 by Darton, Longman & Todd Ltd and Doubleday & Company, Inc.

Part of Chapter II first appeared in *The Tablet* (Nov. 29, 1986) and part of Chapter X first appeared in *Review for Religious* (Jan.–Feb., 1987) and are used here with permission of the editors.

Library of Congress Cataloging-in-Publication Data

Barry, William A.
    Seek my face : prayer as personal relationship in Scripture / William A. Barry
        p.   cm.
    Bibliography: p.
    ISBN 0-8091-3025-4 : $5.95 (est.)
    1.Prayer. 2. Prayer—Biblical teaching. 3. Bible—Criticism, interpretation, etc. 4. Spiritual life—Catholic authors.
I. Title.
BV215.B373 1989
248.3'2—dc19   88-30534
                                                                                    CIP

Published by Paulist Press
997 Macarthur Boulevard
Mahwah, New Jersey 07430

Printed and bound in the
United States of America

To My Good Friends

Patricia Y. Geoghegan and
Joseph E. McCormick, S.J.

With Love and Gratitude

Contents

Preface

This little book on prayer is a sequel to *God and You: Prayer as a Personal Relationship* which appeared in 1987. Like that book this one too is based on experience, my own and that of many others who have talked to me about their experience of God. Like that one this too is based in the Ignatian tradition which uses scripture imaginatively to let the person encounter God. In this book I take up various scriptural incidents and personalities to illustrate various ways of developing an intimate relationship with God, with God's Son, Jesus, and with God's Holy Spirit. My hope is to help at least some people to enter more deeply that relationship which grounds our very existence in this world.

While scripture forms the base from which I work, I have to admit that I am not a scripture scholar. I have tried to be faithful to the texts, but my method might be called eisegesis rather than exegesis. In other words, I read into the text more than the author intended. Such a method has an honorable tradition in the history of Christianity and Judaism. An example is the way in which the Song of Songs has been used to describe the relation of a person to God. Another example is provided by the way Ignatius of Loyola invites the retreatant to contemplate the gospels in the *Spiritual Exercises.* Readers who are looking for careful scriptural exegesis to understand passages are referred to such works as *The Jerome Biblical Commentary* or to commentaries on the various books of the bible.

Once again I want to remark on my use of the masculine gender for God. I have kept to the traditional usage even though God is neither male nor female. However, I have used the *New International Version* which seems to try for a more inclusive language and also eliminates the formal Thee and Thou for God. Moreover, for the psalms I have used *Psalms Anew In Inclusive Language*. And in my own writing I have tried to minimize usage that disturbs and offends many women.

I have dedicated this book to Patricia Y. Geoghegan and Joseph E. McCormick, S.J., both of whom have been friends for many years and have read my manuscripts with great care, attention to detail, and encouragement. Both of them have been especially helpful with this book. "Thanks" seems too small a word for all that I owe them.

I also want to thank the following members of my community who read most or all of this book as I wrote it and were so helpful and encouraging: Robert Araujo, N.S.J., James L. Burke, S.J., Gerald Calhoun, S.J., Gregory Chisholm, S.J., William Finneran, S.J., Thomas Ford, N.S.J., Robert Gilroy, N.S.J., James Kane, S.J., Thomas Landy, N.S.J., Daniel Merrigan, S.J., Thomas Murphy, N.S.J., William Spokesfield, S.J., Michael Toth, N.S.J., and George Williams, N.S.J. Once again Philomena Sheerin, M.M.M. has read the manuscript carefully and by her enthusiasm boosted my confidence in its worth. I want to thank my former provincial, Edward M. O'Flaherty, S.J. and my present one, Robert E. Manning, S.J., for missioning me to write and for their confidence in me. Finally I thank all those who have entrusted to me their experiences of God. If this book is helpful to others, it is due, under God, to these people who enlarged my own understanding of God's ways. If the reader finds help in these pages, please offer a prayer for all the people who have made it possible for me to write them and, of course, for me.

Chapter I

Our Ambivalence About God

Intimacy with God. What could that mean? In a series of chapters based on bible stories I would like to flesh out an answer to this question. For beginning purposes let us assume that intimacy means a close personal relationship. This definition itself raises at least one issue immediately, our ambivalence about such a relationship with God.

When we hear someone say, "I want a closer relationship with God," many of us may react as did a woman quoted in *The Practice of Spiritual Direction* when she heard something similar: "In my time we wanted to be on the right side of him, but we didn't want to get too close." We may smile at the remark, but most of us, with a bit of honesty, would say that any desire for closeness to God we have is tempered by our fear of what such closeness might entail. One of the least controvertible statements we can make about our relationship with God (from our side) is that it is a highly ambivalent one, an approach-avoidance dance, as it were.

The words of the Israelites in the desert to Moses may typify at least part of our attitude toward God: "Speak to us yourself and we will listen. But do not have God speak to us or we will die" (Ex 20:19). Yet at the same time we may be moved by the words of the Psalmist:

Hear me when I cry aloud;
be gracious to me and answer me!
You have said, "Seek my face."
My heart says to you, "Your face I do seek.
Do not hide your face from me." (Ps 27:7–9)

In this chapter I want to discuss this ambivalence toward God, and ways of dealing with it in prayer.

If you have read this far, you have demonstrated an interest in God and in prayer. There are many people with such an interest these days. Books on prayer sell well, and workshops and talks on prayer draw well. Many people seem to desire to see the face of God more clearly. On the other hand, anyone who gives spiritual direction can attest to a persistent resistance to a closer relationship with God in everyone who desires such closeness. Even after, indeed sometimes especially after very positive experiences of God's closeness, people find themselves unaccountably reluctant to continue such types of prayer. We seem condemned to efforts to avoid the very thing we want. It might help to look at some of the sources of our resistance.

Many people who desire a closer relationship with God have an image of God that makes closeness difficult. For example, whether it derives from childhood relationships with parents or other authority figures or from the way God was presented and/or the way the child understood the presentation, an image of God as a demanding, harsh, all-knowing taskmaster cannot sustain a desire for closeness with God. If such a subconscious image dominates a person's vision of God, homilies and even testimonies about God's loving kindness, while they may evoke a desire to know God differently, will not make possible a real openness to closeness to such a God.

Many people resist closeness to God because they fear

that such closeness will require a change in their life style or a more radical religiousness or a conversion. "If I get close to God, he will see right through me and require change." "What if God wants me to become a missionary!" Fears such as these may come from the kind of image of God mentioned in the last paragraph, but they also may be a sign of some unease about present life style or behavior. Whatever their source, such fears inhibit closeness.

People resist closeness to Jesus often enough because of realistic fears that they may get the same treatment he received. "If any one would come after me, he must deny himself and take up his cross and follow me" (Mk 8:34). Taking these words seriously would daunt any sane person.

Finally, and perhaps most deeply, there seems to be in each of us a profound fear that closeness to God will destroy us. The Israelites voiced that fear to Moses. At the beginning of chapter 6 the prophet Isaiah has a vision of God and then says: "Woe to me! I am ruined! For I am a man of unclean lips, and I live among a people of unclean lips, and my eyes have seen the King, the Lord Almighty" (Is 6:5).

These sources of resistance sit deep within us, and they cannot be wished or willed away. Are we then condemned to a lifetime of desiring closeness to God and of doing everything in our power to prevent such closeness? Reflection on these scripture texts and on our human relationships may show us a way to proceed out of this impasse.

The Israelites and Isaiah obviously were aware of their reactions to God's closeness. So the first piece of advice is: pay attention to your real feelings, reactions and thoughts about God. We cannot become aware of all of our reactions all at once, but we can advert to some of them. Just as obviously, the Israelites and Isaiah voiced what they felt. Here is the crux of the matter. If the Israelites had not told Moses how afraid they were, they would not have heard him say: "Do not be afraid. God has come to test you, so that the fear of God will be with you to keep you from sinning" (Ex 20:20). Their fear was not taken away, but the writer seems to indicate that it was eased enough so that they could stand at a distance while Moses entered the thick cloud. In the beginning that may be the best that we can do ourselves, that is, voice our fear and then stand at a bit of a distance to see what happens.

In the case of Isaiah the response comes directly from the Lord. "Then one of the seraphs flew to me with a live coal in his hand, which he had taken with tongs from the altar. With it he touched my mouth and said, 'See, this has touched your lips; your guilt is taken away and your sin atoned for' " (Is 6:6–7). Isaiah, it seems, is so transformed by this experience that he now responds eagerly, "Here I am. Send me," when he hears the Lord say, "Whom shall I send? And who will go for us?" (Is 6:8).

If we are aware that we are, for whatever reason, afraid of God, then we can voice that fear in words like these: "God, I'm terrified of you; can you help me get over the fear?" If I find that I cannot really believe that God is love, I can tell him so: "The bible says that you are love, but I have never experienced you that way. Help me out of this dilemma." "I want to experience your love, but I'm afraid; don't scare me." "Jesus called you Papa (Abba); I'd like to feel that way about you too, but I don't." "I want to get closer to you, but I'm afraid of what you'll ask of me." "I'm so full of anger about my mother's death that I don't know what to do with myself. I'm afraid that you will punish me for feeling this way. Help me."

Notice that these little prayers express the ambivalence simply and straightforwardly. The person says what he/she is afraid of and what he/she wants. The next step is up to God. All we can do is give him a chance to respond by either sitting quietly, or reading a scripture text, or taking a walk in the woods, or doing anything that gets our minds off ourselves and our own concerns for a little while.

What reflection on these scripture texts has recommended to us can also be reinforced by a consideration of any personal relationship. If I want to get to know you better but am afraid of you for some reason, the best way around the impasse is for me to tell you what I'm feeling and ask your help. You may be offended by my feeling afraid or by my forwardness and tell me to get lost, but we have abundant evidence in scripture that God does not act that way. "Can a mother forget the baby at her breast and have no compassion on the child she has borne? Though she may forget, I will not forget you. See, I have engraved you on the palms of my hands" (Is 49:15–16). In fact, you, like most human beings, probably will be disarmed by my candor and even flattered that I want to get to know you better and trust you enough to speak honestly. My fear of you will only be overcome by my experience of you. The very same thing is true of our relationship with God. Our faulty images of him will only be changed by our experience of him. Isaiah found out by experience that he could "see" God and live, and this experience then led him to respond positively to God's invitation to undertake a mission. More than likely our own relationship with God will not shift so rapidly from fear to companionship, but even the first step of telling God how we feel about him is a step toward a deeper intimacy because we have revealed something of ourselves.

Some readers may be helped, as I have been, to express their ambivalence to God by this prayerful sonnet of John Donne.

> Batter my heart, three-personed God; for You
> As yet but knock, breathe, shine, and seek to mend;
> That I may rise and stand, o'erthrow me, and bend

Your force to break, blow, burn, and make me new.
I, like an usurped town, to another due,
Labour to admit You, but O, to no end;
Reason, Your viceroy in me, me should defend,
But is captived, and proves weak or untrue.
Yet dearly I love You, and would be loved fain,
But am betrothed unto Your enemy:
Divorce me, untie, or break that knot again;
Take me to You, imprison me, for I
Except You enthrall me, never shall be free,
Nor ever chaste, except you ravish me.

Chapter II

Feeling Accepted: The Foundational Experience

With all our ambivalence about closeness to God, how do we take the first step? What will so involve us with God that we will stay with the relationship even when the fears and anxieties are very strong? Experience tells us that we only risk intimacy with another when love for the other is stronger than our fears. The first letter of John tells us: "And so we know and rely on the love God has for us. God is love. Whoever lives in love lives in God, and God in him. . . . There is no fear in love. But perfect love drives out fear. . . . We love because he first loved us" (1 Jn 4:16–19). Here we have the clue we need. In order to overcome our ambivalence we need a deep experience of how God has loved us first. We need, in other words, an experience that will elicit from our hearts that lovely phrase, *Qu'il est bon, le bon Dieu* (How good he is, the good God). But how do we attain that experience, especially if our fears are quite strong?

First, let us turn to a non-biblical source to begin to approximate an answer. In Antoine de Saint-Exupéry's *The Little Prince* the little prince from asteroid B-612 meets a fox on our earth and learns from the fox what friendship means. The fox asks the prince to "tame him," that is, "to establish ties." "I want to, very much. . . . But I have not much time. I have friends to discover, and a great many things to understand," says the little prince. "One only understands the things that one tames," replies the fox; that is, one only really understands what one loves or has befriended. He then tells the little prince that he must be very patient if he wants to tame him. "First you will sit down at a little distance from me—like that—in the grass. I shall look at you out of the corner of my eye, and you will say nothing. Words are the source of misunderstandings. But you will sit a little closer to me, every day. . . ." And so begins the process of taming, of establishing ties, between the fox and the little prince.

As we begin to desire a deeper and closer relationship with God, we may be as skittish as the fox. We need to be tamed by the Lord. We can begin as simply as does the fox by asking the Lord to "tame" us, to spend time with us each day, but slowly so that we get used to his presence. The fox also tells the little prince that rites are important, and suggests that they set aside a time each day when the little prince can come. We can do the same with God and make the time as long or as short as we wish or are able.

When we are feeling skittish and afraid, what do we desire? We want to experience God as gentle, caring, loving, attractive, indeed, as desiring our friendship. We want to enjoy God and thus feel safe, as the British psychiatrist, J. S. Mackenzie, puts it. He is cited by the psychoanalyst Henry Guntrip who goes on to say: "It is a common experience in psychotherapy to find patients who fear and hate God, a God who, in the words of J. S. Mackenzie 'is always snooping around after sinners'. . ." Anyone who has done pastoral work can say that it is a common experience to find many Christians like this. And while sermons and homilies whose theme is the love of God may help, ultimately people need to experience that love.

In his insightful book, *Let This Mind Be In You*, Sebastian Moore leads one to the conclusion that if we could experience our creation we would experience in absolute fashion how desirable we are. God's desire for me makes me to be, indeed, to be desirable. With us what is lovely arouses our desire; with God his desire (love) creates what is lovely. So his desire creates me lovely, i.e., desirable. The question is: can we experience our creation? On the face of it the question seems absurd because almost automatically we think of creation as something over and done with. But God's creative act is never done; if it were, we would not be. With such an understanding of creation the question takes on present meaning. If we could experience our creation, then indeed we would have the foundational experience we are seeking.

Moore points to experiences of a welling up of desire for "I know not what." The desire is not for this or that lovely being although the occasion for the experience may be the presence of some lovely being. The desire is for the unnameable, the "All," the Mystery. Moore refers to an experience described by C. S. Lewis in his autobiography, *Suprised by Joy:*

> As I stood before a flowering currant bush on a summer day there suddenly arose in me without warning, and as if from a depth not of years but of centuries, the memory of that earlier morning at the Old House when my brother had brought his toy garden into the nursery. It is difficult to find words strong enough for the sensation which came over me; Milton's "enormous bliss" of Eden . . . comes somewhere near it. It was a sensation, of course, of desire; but desire for what? not, certainly, for a biscuit tin filled

with moss, nor even (though that came into it) for my own past. . . . and before I knew what I desired, the desire itself was gone, the whole glimpse withdrawn, the world turned commonplace again, or only stirred by a longing for the longing that had just ceased. It had taken only a moment of time; and in a certain sense everything else that had ever happened to me was insignificant in comparison.

This experience of desire is actually the Joy that surprised Lewis.

Recently I had an experience that seemed to be of the same "stuff," as it were. I was walking outside on a lovely, clear, crisp, autumn day by the shore. I admired the sun on the autumn leaves and on the blue water. Suddenly there welled up in me a feeling of great well-being and a strong desire for "I know not what," for the "All," for union, that made me very happy. I remembered a few other times of such joy and desire and realized why autumn is my favorite season—because it is associated in memory with such experiences. Almost as quickly as it came it was gone. I was happy afterwards, not downcast that I no longer had the experience. I would like to have the experience again, but I am not bereft without it. Later that week in a class I recounted the experience, and many in the class acknowledged having similar experiences. I wonder if these are not experiences of our creation.

God, as Moore says, is the only one who can directly touch the core of our desirableness. His desire makes us desirable, makes us "the apple of his eye." It would be strange indeed if we never experienced that core reality. In the experience I had there was, besides the desire for "I know not what," the "All," a sense of personal well-being. I felt good about myself insofar as I thought of myself at all. So it does not seem odd to think of the experience as an experience of my creation. Nor is it strange that such experiences are intermittent and fleeting. Our tendency is to pay more attention to what is happening at the surface of our being than to what is going on in our depths. Moreover, we have learned not to put too much stock in experiences that might "turn our heads," "make us proud." Moore equates original sin with those elements in our culture and families that press us to deny our loveliness, to repress the memory of what Lewis calls Joy, the memory of the experience of being desired into being and of thus desiring "we know not what." We may be not only surprised by Joy, but also awed or terrified by it. Ambivalence is ever-present in our closest relationships and should, therefore, be expected in the most intimate of all, our relationship with God. Thus, for many reasons these experiences of our creation will seem evanescent. Yet do they not leave us recalling that our hearts burned within us as did the hearts of the two disciples who met the risen Lord on the road to Emmaus?

If we take such experiences seriously, we will understand how Augustine could say: "My heart is restless until it rests in Thee." Moore indicates that the creative touch of God rouses my desirableness which in turn sets off my desire for "I know not what." Like Augustine C. S. Lewis sought to assuage that desire in any number of ways, but none of them proved to be "I know not what." Ultimately they found that Joy was the desire for the Mystery we call God. Rudolph Otto's Holy, the attractive and awesome One, is the lovely one who is the deepest object of all our desiring. I believe that such an experience of our creation is the affective first principle and foundation upon which any development of a personal relationship with God must rest.

There is a wonderful story in the book of Exodus that can also serve as a help to overcome our fears. Moses and the people of Israel are in the desert.

Moses said to the Lord, "You have been telling me, 'Lead these people,' but you have not let me know whom you will send with me. You have said, 'I know you by name and you have found favor with me.' If you are pleased with me, teach me your ways so I may know you and continue to find favor with you. Remember that this nation is your people." The Lord replied, "My Presence will go with you, and I will give you rest." Then Moses said to him, "If your Presence does not go with us, do not send us up from here. How will anyone know that you are pleased with me and with your people unless you go with us? What else will distinguish me and your people from all other people on the face of the earth?" And the Lord said to Moses, "I will do the very thing you have asked, because I am pleased with you and I know you by name." Then Moses said, "Now show me your glory." And the Lord said, "I will cause all my goodness to pass in front of you, and I will proclaim my name, the Lord, in your presence. I will have mercy on whom I will have mercy, and I will have compassion on whom I will have compassion. But," he said, "you cannot see my face, for no one may see me and live." Then the Lord said, "There is a place near me where you may stand on a rock. When my glory passes by, I will put you in a cleft in the rock and cover you with my hand until I have passed by. Then I will remove my hand, and you shall see my back; but my face must not be seen." (Ex 33:12–23)

First, notice that Moses makes known to God what he wants. He takes God at his word, "If you are pleased with me, teach me your ways. . . ." The first reason Moses adduces to obtain what he wants is personal. "You say that you love me; then show me." The second is also interesting, "Remember that this nation is your people." In other words, "Show me your ways also for the sake of the people you ask

me to lead." Each one of us can count on the same arguments to induce God to reveal himself as gracious to us.
God has made each one of us because he desired us as his
children; so we can remind him of this even using Moses'
words. Moreover, each of us is responsible for others, in
relationship to others who are also God's children, his people. We can also use Moses' second argument. "If I'm less
afraid of you, more in love with you, I'll be a better mother,
father, friend, co-worker, parishioner, community member,
etc."

Then notice the tender concern of God. He knows that
we are limited in our ability to tolerate closeness to him.
"No one may see me and live." I am reminded of the
poignant-sounding phrase Ignatius of Loyola uses in the
Spiritual Exercises:

> I will ponder with great affection how much God our Lord
> has done for me, and how much He has given of what He
> possesses, and finally, how much, *as far as He can,* the
> same Lord desires to give Himself to me according to His
> divine decrees.

The words I have italicized are the ones that sound so poignant, as though God would like to give us more of himself,
but cannot because of our limitations. So God says to Moses, "I will cover you with my hand until I have passed by."
He will protect his friend from whatever dangers there are in
closeness to him. What a touching thing for God to say and
do!

Finally, we note who God says he is: the Lord who will
have mercy on whom he will have mercy. We want to experience him as gracious to us, "the compassionate and gracious
God, slow to anger, abounding in love and faithfulness"
(Gen 34:6).

It would seem that God knows how skittish we are and

tailors his presence to our ability and desire to tolerate it. If, like the fox, we ask him to be present, but at a respectable distance, so that we can gradually get used to him, he, it seems, will abide by our wishes. One gets the impression that God will do whatever is necessary to prove to us that he really is "Abba," dear father, dear mother, for us. He wants us to believe that and to let him come close. Not even the murder of his Son Jesus could change his mind and heart. We need an experience of such a God to involve us in the relationship so strongly that we will let God overcome our fears.

Chapter III

Growing Transparency

One of the more endearing images of intimacy between human beings and God occurs in the book of Genesis right after disaster has struck. In 3:8 we read, "Then the man and his wife heard the sound of the Lord God as he was walking in the garden in the cool of the day. . . ." One gets the impression that this walk in the garden was a common event in the mind of the writer of the narrative. We are invited to imagine God walking with Adam and Eve, enjoying the wonders of creation, the way three old and good friends might walk around a lovely garden. But this evening a new element has entered in; Adam and Eve have eaten the forbidden fruit. ". . . and they hid from the Lord God among the trees of the garden. But the Lord God called to the man, 'Where are you?' He answered, 'I heard you in the garden, and I was afraid because I was naked; so I hid' " (Gen 3:8–10). The intimacy has been disrupted. The disruption is symbolized by the man's new fear of being naked before God. "I hid." Where before nothing was hidden from God, not even one's most intimate bodily parts, now the man and the woman try to hide themselves from God. In *Drawn to the Divine* William Reiser entitles his first chapter "Adam in Hiding" and notes that we are all in hiding, "running away from intimacy with

God as Adam did." Transparency between humans and God, once, it seems, so effortlessly present, becomes painful and very difficult.

In the first chapter we discussed some ways of overcoming this ambivalence. In this one I want to take up at more length the issue of transparency as it bears on our relationship with God. We are still circling around the question of what intimacy with God might mean.

The chapters (4 to 11) of Genesis after the fall depict a world where humans are progressively more estranged from God and finally even from one another. The human estrangement is symbolized in chapter 11 by the confusion of languages introduced at Babel. The Abraham stories that begin in chapter 12 can be seen as a new beginning. Eugene Maly (in *The Jerome Biblical Commentary*) notes: "The mounting (aversion from God) that characterized the first 11 chapters now gives way to a (conversion to God)." I want to use some of the Abraham stories to illustrate what a growing intimacy with God might look like from the side of the human being.

In what follows I will be using the biblical text as an opportunity to reflect on our relationship with God. In the process we will be reading into the text more than the authors of the original stories and the final author or authors intended. I hope that we will not be doing violence to the text, but rather reading it prayerfully and respectfully for nourishment for our lives of prayer.

The story opens with God's word to Abram:

> Leave your country, your people and your father's household and go to the land that I will show you. I will make you into a great nation and I will bless you; I will make your name great, and you will be a blessing. I will bless those who bless you, and whoever curses you I will curse;

and all peoples on earth will be blessed through you. (Gen 12:1–3).

Abram's response is to go into an unknown land. In the ensuing three chapters God repeats his promise to bless Abram. Only in the fifteenth chapter do we hear Abram responding verbally to God's promise. He wants to know how God's promise will be fulfilled since he is childless by his wife Sarai. God promises that he will have a son by Sarai. Abram asks for a sign, and God grants his request.

Let us pause here and reflect. As the text stands Abram's first response to God's initiative is blind, unquestioning obedience and trust. Only later when he and Sarai continue childless does the question come, "How will the promises come about?" Abram does not quash the question. He puts it to God and God responds. Abram still has a doubt and so he asks for a sign, and again God responds. Here we see one essential for a growing intimacy with God, the willingness to communicate to God what relating to him does to me. If I do not understand his ways with me or do not like them, I must be willing to try to reveal myself to God if I want a closer relationship with him. Only by revealing his doubts and questions does Abram find out how seriously God wants his belief and trust.

In this regard it might be good to remind ourselves what happens to any personal relationship when I withhold from the other what the other's words or deeds are doing to me. Suppose that you tell me that you love me, but I find that hard to believe because you do not take any initiative in the relationship, leaving it all up to me. If I do not tell you what I am feeling, then our relationship is in danger of becoming polite and formal and distant. Abram did not take this route.

In the seventeenth chapter some new elements enter this developing relationship. Abram is now ninety-nine years old and Sarai is eighty-nine. God reveals who he is, "I am God Almighty" (1) and Abram falls on his face, presumably in adoration. God then renews his promises and changes Abram's name to Abraham, "for I have made you the father of many nations" (5). God promises to be God to this great people which Abraham will father. Later he says, "As for Sarai your wife, you are no longer to call her Sarai, her name will be Sarah. I will bless her and will surely give you a son by her" (15–16). In some languages, French and German for example, developing intimacy is signaled by the change from a formal address to the use of first names and the intimate forms of "you." It may not be far fetched to read such a process into this process of name changing.

Another indication of the change in the quality of the relationship occurs right after God's promise about Sarah. "Abraham fell face-down; he laughed and said to himself, 'Will a son be born to a man a hundred years old? Will Sarah bear a child at the age of ninety?' And Abraham said to God, 'If only Ishmael' (his son by Hagar) 'might live under your blessing!' " (17–18). In the middle of his prayer (his conversation with God) Abraham has a belly laugh about what God is promising and then gets practical. "If I'm going to be the father of many nations, it can only be through Ishmael. So I want you to bless him." How does God respond? He does not get angry or upset, it seems, but responds to the point. "Yes, but your wife Sarah will bear you a son, and you will call him Isaac. I will establish my covenant with him as an everlasting convenant for his descendants after him" (19). But that is not the end of the response. He goes on to say: "And as for Ishmael, I have heard you; I will surely bless him; I will make him fruitful. . . . But my covenant I will establish with Isaac, whom Sarah will bear to you by this time next year" (20–21).

It seems that Abraham is getting bolder in his conversations with the Lord. He can now laugh at what God says and even make jokes about it. And he can, in effect, tell God to be practical. And God responds in kind. One can almost hear a smile in the words, "And as for Ishmael, I have heard you."

A similar scene is repeated in chapter 18 where the Lord again appears to Abraham. (That several traditions are joined together in this chapter is indicated by the uncertainty of who appears, e.g., "the Lord," "three men," "they said," "he said." In a later chapter we shall return to this passage when we discuss how God is experienced by people.) Abraham invites his guest(s) to a meal with customary Middle Eastern hospitality. In the course of this dinner around the campfire God asks about Sarah and then promises that when he returns in the spring Sarah will have a son. Sarah is listening at the tent door and she laughs to herself, saying, "After I am worn out and my master is old, will I now have this pleasure?" (12). The Lords asks Abraham, "Why did Sarah laugh . . ?" (13). He then repeats his promise, and Sarah denies laughing because she is afraid. But God just says, "Yes, you did laugh" (15). One has the impression of a bantering conversation between friends, and even Sarah's fear at the end seems easily handled by the Lord.

This scene then fades into the next where the Lord tells Abraham that he intends to destroy Sodom and Gomorrah. "Shall I hide from Abraham what I am about to do? Abraham will surely become a great and powerful nation, and all nations on earth will be blessed through him. For I have chosen him . . ." (17–19). It would seem that God, too, is becoming more transparent with Abraham as Abraham becomes more open with him. When the Lord does reveal what he intends to do, Abraham draws near and begins to haggle with God and even reminds God of who God is. "Will you sweep away the righteous with the wicked? What if there are fifty righteous people in the city? Will you sweep it away and not spare the place for the sake of the fifty righteous people in it? Far be it from you to do such a thing—to kill the righteous with the wicked, treating the righteous and the wicked alike. Far be it from you! Will not the Judge of all the earth do right?" (23–25). If you can imagine speaking to the Lord of the universe in this fashion, you can probably feel yourself flinch in anticipation of God's wrath. Yet we all know what happens. Instead of getting angry, God agrees about the fifty and then the bargaining begins. Finally God agrees that he will not destroy Sodom if he finds ten righteous people within the city and they part company.

We may be tempted to say that such intimacy was fine for Abraham, but it is not for the likes of us. Yet we need to remind ourselves that these biblical stories are told to reveal what God is like. It would appear that God is pleased with the openness, the transparency Abraham developed. Such a developing transparency shows a growing trust in God so that by the end of this cycle of stories Abraham can say whatever comes to mind and know that he is heard. If God was pleased with Abraham's growing trust, perhaps he will be equally pleased with our fumbling efforts. It is worth a try as another step toward overcoming our fear of closeness to God, or, to put it positively, as another step toward satisfying our desire for a closer relationship with God.

Chapter IV

Hearing God

In the third chapter we looked at the growing intimacy between Abraham and God. There we concentrated on what seemed Abraham's developing willingness and ability to reveal more and more of himself to God. We noted that Abraham seemed to become gradually more willing to be transparent before God. But we also became aware that God took the initiative in the relationship and that he revealed himself to Abraham more and more openly. The process culminated in God's revelation of his intention to destroy Sodom and Gomorrah, a revelation which led Abraham to confront God directly and haggle with him. Some of us may, perhaps, have wondered about these revelations of God and especially about whether and how God reveals himself to us.

The bible records many words of God to individuals and groups. God speaks to Adam and Eve in the garden both before and after the fall. He speaks to Cain after the murder of Abel, to Noah to warn him of the coming flood, to Noah and his sons after the flood, and many times to Abraham and Sarah. He speaks to Moses and Aaron and Miriam, to the prophets, to David and Solomon, and to many others. In the New Testament God speaks through Gabriel, the archangle, to Mary and Zechariah, in a dream to Joseph, and directly to Jesus. And Jesus after his death speaks to Mary, to Peter, to all the disciples, and, after the ascension, to Paul. The question that must come if we are to talk about our intimacy with God and with Jesus and with the Spirit is: does God reveal himself directly to us and if so, how?

Let's return to that endearing image of Genesis 3, God walking with the man and the woman in the garden in the cool of the day. What are we to make of this image? After all God does not have a body. Obviously then God did not walk in the garden the way you and I walk. Adam and Eve could have held hands and looked at one another, but their awareness of God's presence had to be different. No matter how privileged their intimacy with God may have been, that intimacy had to be mediated in some way through their senses, their imaginations, their feelings and their thoughts. In other words, their experience of God, like ours, is also "experience of something else at the same time" as John E. Smith says in *Experience and God*. It is important that we grasp this idea lest we consciously or subconsciously make the experience of biblical heroes and of saints of a different order than our own and thus out of our reach and understanding.

Recall the revelation that Isaiah describes at the beginning of his sixth chapter, the one that so terrified him. He has a vision of the Lord and the heavenly court. When he cries out in fear, one of the seraphs flies toward him and with a burning coal touches his lips and tells him that his guilt is taken away. Then he hears the voice of the Lord, "Whom shall I send? And who will go for us?" to which Isaiah replies, "Here I am. Send me" (Is 6:8). Isaiah has had a powerful experience of God; that is undeniable. But in trying to describe his experience he uses images with which he and his readers are familiar, the throne, the seraphim, the smoke, etc. We can speculate that in the experience itself these same images were at work in Isaiah. That is, we can say that God used Isaiah's imagination (which was conditioned by all that he had seen, heard, read and felt in his life) to communicate to Isaiah his vocation.

There is no other way for human beings to experience God than through their human consciousness. God, as our creator and continuing creator, can and does touch us at the heart of our being. As Sebastian Moore says, God's desire for me makes me to be and to be desirable, and that creative touch is experienced every so often. We are "surprised by joy" in the words of C. S. Lewis. But in experiencing that touch we also experience something else at the same time, e.g., a warm human touch, sunlight on leaves, a memory, an image, an unbidden thought. So too, we have experiences analogous to that of Isaiah when the awesomeness of God's felt presence fills us with both longing and dread. Perhaps it occurred in a church when architecture, silence, incense all contributed to the experience of being in the presence of the Holy Mystery.

In his autobiographical memoir *The Sacred Journey* Frederick Buechner recalls an incident that he believed was the revelatory touch of God. His mother had taken him and his brother to Bermuda to live after his father's tragic suicide. Near the end of their two-year stay he was sitting at dusk with a thirteen year old girl when their bare knees happened to touch for a moment. ". . . and in that moment," he says, "I was filled with such a sweet panic and anguish of longing for I had no idea what that I knew my life could never be complete until I found it." He cannot deny that the feelings can be explained psychologically, yet, he says, ". . . I choose not to deny, either, the compelling sense of an unseen giver and a series of hidden gifts as not only another part of their reality, but the deepest part of all" (pp. 51–56). We have looked at experiences like this in Chapter II. The point here is that we, too, may have had experiences similar to the one

Isaiah describes, even if less powerful in their imagery and import. God has made his creative mystery known to us in our human experience.

We can make the same point by looking at the stories of Abraham and Sarah. Again we remind ourselves that these are stories told centuries after the events they are supposed to be recounting. We cannot be sure what the historical Abraham and Sarah experienced, but we can use the stories to gather some insight into the mystery of God's ways with us. Thus if Abram "hears" God telling him to leave his home to go into an unknown land, it must be through an imagined voice, an "inner voice" as it were. That inner voice would be conditioned by all that he has heard in life. Insofar as it is religious, it would be conditioned by all the stories he had heard of God. Some people do hear such an inner voice with distinct words and sentences. Others, however, would describe what happens to them as more a feeling for what was being communicated; e.g., "I felt that God was pleased with me, was telling me that he loved me," or "I sensed that God was asking me whether I would preach his word as Isaiah did."

Let us now return to chapter 18 of Genesis. "The Lord appeared to Abraham near the great trees of Mamre while he was sitting at the entrance to his tent in the heat of the day. Abraham looked up and saw three men standing nearby" (Gen 18:1–2). Recall that later in the scene the text shifts from "they said" to "the Lord said" within the same conversation (vv 9–10). The final editor of the text has probably melded different traditions, one of which spoke of the vision of one person, another of three persons. But both images clearly represent the Lord. The pattern of the story is a familiar one. A stranger or strangers appear, the surprised resident receives them graciously and hospitably, and they turn out to be either emissaries of God or God himself. Without wanting to imply that such a "natural" explanation exhausts the meaning of the story, I invite the reader to reflect on whether something similar has happened. Have you ever come away from a chance meeting with a stranger and felt powerfully moved, excited and alive, somehow aware of having "met the Lord" in this encounter? One's life could be changed forever by the event.

In my own life something like this happened. I was nearing the end of my sophomore year in college. The idea of joining the Jesuits had been with me since freshman year, but I had decided to hold off at least until I had finished college. Indeed, at a lecture given by a famous layman I recall thinking that I could do as much good for people as a layman as I would as a Jesuit. I was studying for final exams with a friend, and at the end of the evening he told me—to my complete surprise—that he had applied to enter the Jesuits that summer. As I walked home, I said to myself, "If he can do it, why can't I?" and began the process of application two days later. Both of us entered the Jesuits on the same day two months later. Of course, there were a lot of influences at work, but, like Buechner, I choose to see also the finger of God in the experience. And it has profoundly affected my life.

Buechner's memoir provides another example. Not long after his first novel was published, a minister he scarcely knew asked him to lunch. They had little in common and in the course of the conversation Buechner began to wonder what the point was. But then the conversation switched, and the minister was talking about Buechner's gift.

> Had I ever considered, he said, putting my gift for words to work for—God, did he say? Or the church? or Christ? I no longer remember how he put it exactly, and he made no great thing of it but passed on soon to other matters so that

I do not to this day know whether this was what he had asked me to lunch to say or not. . . . And that was the end of it except that out of all the events that took place during those five years of teaching at Lawrenceville, it is one of the few that I remember distinctly, like an old photograph preserved by accident between the pages of a book. (p. 101)

Buechner, who had no intention of such a career, is now a Presbyterian minister whose sermons and books have touched many lives. Perhaps we, too, have met a stranger, and, like the two disciples who met the stranger on the way to Emmaus, have felt "our hearts burning within us" while talking with him or her (Lk 24:32). If so, then we have an experience of the way God communicates to us through the people we meet as well as through the events of our lives.

There is a marvelous story of how God was experienced in nature by the prophet Elijah. In 1 Kings 19 Elijah has reached Mount Horeb and lodged in a cave. The Lord says to him:

"Go out and stand on the mountain in the presence of the Lord, for the Lord is about to pass by." Then a great and powerful wind tore the mountains apart and shattered the rocks before the Lord, but the Lord was not in the wind. After the wind there was an earthquake, but the Lord was not in the earthquake. After the earthquake came a fire, but the Lord was not in the fire. And after the fire came a gentle whisper. When Elijah heard it, he pulled his cloak over his face and went out and stood at the mouth of the cave. (1Kgs 19:11–13)

Often enough people do feel that God speaks directly to them in the wonders of nature. A sunset may not only arouse in me feelings of delight, but also of awe, and I may spontaneously praise God because I sense his presence. The power of a storm can evoke a sense of God's power. The play of light and shadow in a forest can draw us into a sense of the mysterious presence of God. And—as with Elijah—a gentle breeze on our face can fill us with warmth, a feeling that we have been caressed by the Almighty One who is gentle as a mother with a child or a lover with the beloved.

Let me end this essay with another quote from Frederick Buechner: "It seemed to me then, and seems to me still, that if God speaks to us at all in this world, if God speaks anywhere, it is into our personal lives that he speaks." What we need to develop is a contemplative attitude that learns how to notice God when he speaks into our personal lives.

Chapter V

Revealing Our Needs

"All life is suffering." This is the first of the Four Noble Truths of Buddha. M. Scott Peck begins his very influential best seller, *The Road Less Traveled*, with a paraphrase of this truth: "Life is difficult." Whether we are optimistic or pessimistic in our attitudes toward life, all of us know days when life is painful indeed, when, perhaps, we feel at the end of our tether. We may have just lost a job unexpectedly or found out that we have cancer or AIDS; we may have just lost a loved one or are facing such a loss; we may just feel depressed and lonely and wonder what life has in store for us; we may feel crushed by a cycle of poverty and see no way out for ourselves or our children; we may feel almost hopeless as we see the poor we hope to serve crushed by the witless greed of absentee landlords or a faceless corporation. Life is difficult and surely brings a great deal of suffering to all of us. In this chapter I propose to indicate ways of bringing our pain and our needs to the attention of God and of listening to God's response.

The reader may already be objecting that it makes no sense to tell God our troubles since he already knows them. The only thing that makes sense is to ask for his help; that is what prayers of petition are for. But if prayer is a personal relationship, the issue is not one of information, but of sharing. I may know that my closest friend is in anguish because of his father's sudden death, but I want him to talk to me about his feelings and reactions because he's my friend. He knows that I know how devastated he is, but he still wants to talk to me about his feelings because he is my friend. Between friends and lovers information is not important, but communication and transparency are. The same truth applies to our relationship with God.

In the first book of Samuel we read of the plight of Hannah, one of the two wives of Elkanah. The other wife, Peninnah, had children, but Hannah had none, and Peninnah regularly taunted Hannah about her childless condition. In spite of Elkanah's avowed love for Hannah, she was miserable whenever they went up to the temple to offer sacrifice to the Lord. This time she got up and went to the temple alone. "In bitterness of soul Hannah wept much and prayed to the Lord" (1 Sam 1:10). In her distress she vowed to the Lord that if she had a son she would give him to the Lord's service. Now Eli, the priest, was sitting nearby and observed her mouth moving.

> Hannah was praying in her heart, and her lips were moving but her voice was not heard. Eli thought she was drunk and said to her, "How long will you keep on getting drunk? Get rid of your wine." "Not so, my Lord," Hannah replied, "I am a woman who is deeply troubled. I have not been drinking wine or beer; I was pouring out my soul to the Lord. Do not take your servant for a wicked woman; I have been praying here out of my great anguish and grief." Eli answered, "Go in peace, and the God of Israel grant you what you have asked of him." She said, "May your servant

find favor in your eyes." Then she went her way and ate
something, and her face was no longer downcast. (1 Sam
1:13–18)

Notice what happens here. Hannah pours out her anguish
and distress to the Lord. She does not just make a petition
and a vow and leave it at that. Rather, it seems, she tells
God all of her troubles. She probably tells him about Elkanah's profession of love, and perhaps how awful she feels
that his love is not enough. Or, perhaps, her fear that that
love will wither if she does not have a child. She also wants
to have a child. She may tell God about the taunts of Peninnah and her own depression or resentment or desire to throt-
tle her. She wants to be heard by a God who cares. Of course,
she does want to have a child, but there is more to it than
that. Otherwise, she would have just made her request over
and over again. It would seem that God is someone to whom
she can pour out her soul in anguish. When she leaves her
prayer, she has only the prayer of Eli as an answer and thus
no guarantee of a child, but she is no longer sad.

It happens that people's troubles are lightened just because they have poured them out to the Lord. Their illness
is not cured, their loved one not brought back to life. But
something has happened to ease their burdens. If you ask
them to describe their experience, they may just say: "I told
God all that I felt, and he seemed to listen with attention
and sympathy. I felt that he understood what I was going
through, and somehow I felt better."

Eli accuses Hannah of being drunk and wants to drive her
away from her place of prayer. Voices in ourselves may also
get in the way of pouring out our soul to the Lord. We may
feel that we must deserve our sufferings because of our sins.
We may tell ourselves that these sufferings are given to us to
make us more dependent on God, or that others suffer more.

We may hear ourselves say that God knows best. These voices tend to keep us from letting God know how we really feel. In this regard the book of Job is instructive.

Job has lost everything, crops, goods, cattle, and finally his children. His own body is covered with sores. In the presence of his three friends Job curses the day of his birth in a powerful prayer which ends, "For sighing comes to me instead of food; my groans pour out like water. What I feared has come upon me; what I dreaded has happened to me. I have no peace, no quietness; I have no rest, but only turmoil" (Job 3:24–26). Instead of comfort or encouragement Job's friends quote the prevailing theology about good and evil and suffering to convince him not to speak out his anguish. They are like the inner voices we just spoke of. Job and his children must be guilty of sin because the innocent never suffer like this, one says. "Blessed is the man whom God corrects; so do not despise the discipline of the Almighty. For he wounds, but he also binds up; he injures, but his hands also heal" (5:17–18). Another tries to dissuade Job from direct talk to God by assuring him that soon everything will be right again. But Job will not take comfort from their words, nor will he be dissuaded from his desire: "But I desire to speak to the Almighty and to argue my case with God" (13:3). "Why do you hide your face and consider me your enemy?" (13:24). In spite of all the arguments of these friends Job will not give up his desire to hear from God directly.

Once I was speaking with a well-known spiritual writer who mentioned that a person he was directing was experiencing a great deal of dryness and darkness in prayer which caused the person considerable pain and upset. He said that he explained to the person that the experience probably was the dark night of the soul. I blurted out, "But that doesn't mean that the person has to like it, that he or she can't tell

God how troubling the distance is." I believe that many of our theological "explanations" for suffering and for darkness in prayer are like the "explanations" of the friends of Job. They do not really get at the issue—which is one of our real relationship with God—and they cut off open dialogue with God. God does not need to be defended from the feelings, the anguish, the terrifying questions which we have toward him and toward life.

Gerald Manley Hopkins, the nineteenth century English Jesuit poet, voiced such feelings in the following sonnet.

> Thou art indeed just, Lord, if I contend
> With thee; but, sir, so what I plead is just.
> Why do sinners' ways prosper? and why must
> Disappointment all I endeavour end?
>   Wert thou my enemy, O thou my friend,
> How wouldst thou worse, I wonder, than thou dost
> Defeat, thwart me? Oh, the sots and thralls of lust
> Do in spare hours more thrive than I that spend,
> Sir, life upon thy cause. See, banks and brakes
> Now, leavèd how thick! lacèd they are again
> With fretty chervil, look, and fresh wind shakes
> Them; birds build—but not I build; no, but strain,
> Time's eunuch, and not breed one work that wakes.
> Mine, O thou lord of life, send my roots rain.

In fact, Job persists in his desire and God does speak to him out of the whirlwind. Chapters 38 to 41 contain God's response. God does not give justifications for what happened to Job. He tells Job over and over who he is—the God of mystery and of creation without whom nothing would be—either for rejoicing or for suffering.

A great deal of ink has been spilled with regard to God's response to Job. It obviously evokes various reactions in readers, and they range the gamut from acceptance to outright rejection. However, if we stay with the book of Job itself, and especially with the relationship between God and Job, we note two things. In spite of what seems an angry tone on God's part Job is still alive and well at the end. Secondly, he seems satisfied. "Then Job replied to the Lord: 'I know that you can do all things; no plan of yours can be thwarted. . . . Surely I spoke of things I did not understand, things too wonderful for me to know. . . . My ears had heard of you but now my eyes have seen you. Therefore I despise myself and repent in dust and ashes' ". (42:1–6). Moreover, God rebukes the three friends of Job, "because you have not spoken of me what is right, as my servant Job has" (42:7), "and the Lord accepted Job's prayer" (42:9). In other words, however we may react from outside of the relationship, Job and God seem to be satisfied with their interaction.

We do well to remember that no human relationship exactly duplicates any other. A pattern of interaction that is not only satisfying but even gratifying in one pair may be unsatisfying for another pair, even when one of the second pair also belongs to the first. So too, each of us may well have a very different relationship with God so that, for example, Job and God are gratified by the relationship they have whereas Hannah and God relate much differently. Each of us must search for the pattern that seems good for God and us.

In fact, God's reaction to human suffering has not always been perceived as the author of Job has portrayed it. God speaks out of the burning bush to Moses: "I have indeed seen the misery of my people in Egypt. I have heard them crying out because of their slave drivers, and I am concerned about their suffering. So I have come down to rescue them from the hand of the Egyptians and to bring them up out of that land into a good and spacious land, a land flowing with milk and honey . . ." (Ex 3:7–8). To the exiled Israelites God says through Isaiah: "Comfort, comfort my people, says your God. Speak tenderly to Jerusalem, and proclaim to her that her hard service had been completed, that her sin has been paid for, that she has received from the Lord's hand double for all her sins" (Is 40:1–2). And again he says: "Listen to me, O house of Jacob, all you who remain of the house of Israel, you whom I have upheld since you were conceived, and have carried since your birth. Even to your old age and gray hairs I am he, I am he who will sustain you. I have made you and I will carry you; I will sustain you and I will rescue you" (Is 46:3–4). Jesus, we believe, is the enfleshment of God, is the human heart of God. Look at how he reacts. "A man with leprosy came to him and begged him on his knees, 'If you are willing, you can make me clean.' Filled with compassion, Jesus reached out his hand and touched the man. 'I am willing,' he said. Be clean' " (Mk 1:40–41). He wept for Lazarus and his grieving sisters, Martha and Mary (Jn 11:35). And sensing the growing storm gathering about him, he drew near to Jerusalem and "he wept over it and said, 'If you, even you, had only known on this day what would bring you peace' " (Lk 19:41–42). In our own moments of shared pain and rage and grief, there can come over us a sense of an enormous sob, as if the universe itself were crying out: "This is not what I intended!" Perhaps we are sensing God's own grief for the pain in the world.

One clean breast of our feelings may not end the matter either. The story of Hannah gave us an indication that she did not content herself with one outburst. She seems to have kept on pouring out her troubles to God. Jesus provides another example and a mind-boggling one at that. In Gethsemane "he began to be deeply distressed and troubled. 'My soul is overwhelmed with sorrow to the point of death,' he said to them. 'Stay here and keep watch.' Going a little farther, he fell to the ground and prayed that if possible the hour might pass from him. 'Abba, Father,' he said, 'everything is possible for you. Take this cup from me. Yet not what I will, but what you will' " (Mk 14:33–36). In this hour of his agony Jesus tells his Father what he feels and desires. If we enter this scene contemplatively, we are almost overwhelmed with fear and pain—that the Son of God experiences so much darkness that *he* wants out, as it were. In this moment of almost total weakness, he musters the strength to say, "Yet not what I will, but what you will." And once through was not enough. Twice more he goes back and repeats the same words. And somehow he gets the strength to go on.

Karl Rahner's words at the end of his meditation on the agony in the garden *(Spiritual Exercises)* provide a fitting focus and conclusion to this chapter.

> We do not have to do very much. We do not have to do more than Jesus did in Gethsemani the night before His death. But if we are able to do that much—and we can only do it with the grace He merited for us in the Garden of Olives—then we are able to do everything. We should ask for this grace again and again.

Chapter VI

Pouring Out One's Heart

And at the ninth hour Jesus cried in a loud voice, 'Eloi, Eloi, lama sabachthani?' which means, 'My God, my God, why have you forsaken me?' " (Mk 15:34). This cry of Jesus from the cross has turned the blood of Christians cold whenever they have really listened to this passage. If the Son of God could feel so desperately bereft, what hope have we for comfort in our dying? "But he is only quoting Psalm 22," some will say, "and that psalm ends up as praise of God. In the midst of his suffering, Jesus, therefore, is experiencing God's comforting presence." Such reasoning does not readily warm the blood that chilled at the loud cry, "My God, my God, why have you forsaken me?" Mark's text is stark in its portrayal of the death scene; it does not readily yield the comfort that we seek, the hope that Jesus was succored by his Abba. But the reference to Psalm 22 does invite us to look at that prayer and may open up another way for us to grow in closeness to God, the theme of this book.

In the last chapter we noted that Hannah poured out her soul to God in her vexation and trouble. She may have been strengthened by her faith and hope in God, but she is still sorely troubled. So too, even if Jesus is praying Psalm 22

aloud, he is voicing anguish indeed. The psalmist's agony is
real enough.

> My God, my God, why have you deserted me?
> Far from my prayer, from the words I cry?

Not only is he in agony, but it is made worse by the seeming
absence of God, by God's silence.

There are times in everyone's life when prayer seems to
bounce off an impenetrable wall. We cry out for some word
of comfort, some feel of warmth, and—nothing happens.
Not only are our troubles sore, but despair lurks at the door
because the universe does not feel "homey," but rather a
cold, vast, inhospitable place. The psalmist seems to be expressing such an experience, and at the moment of the cruci-
fixion Jesus may have felt so too.

But the psalmist does not quit praying. He continues to
pour out his heart. "I call all day, my God, but you never
answer me; all night long I call and cannot rest." He then
reminds God of past favors.

> Yet, Holy One,
> you who make your home in the praises of Israel—
> in you our ancestors put their trust;
> they trusted and you rescued them.
> They called to you for help and were saved;
> they never trusted you in vain.

The psalmist remembers his people's salvation history and
this gives him strength to go on praying. So too, we can
recall our own salvation history, reminding God of what
Jesus promised and also of what God himself has done for us
personally. St. Ignatius reminds people in desolation to remember the former consolations they had and to trust that
God would once again make his presence felt.

The psalmist also details what is happening to him even though God seems absent.

> Yet here I am, now more worm than human,
> scorn of all, jest of the people.
> All who see me jeer at me;
> they toss their heads and sneer:
> "You relied on Yahweh, let Yahweh save you!
> If Yahweh is your friend, let Yahweh rescue you!"

We, too, can say all that is troubling us, and in detail. Even though God seems unhearing, we put our trust in him and pour out our heart.

Once again the psalmist reminds God and himself of their past relationship.

> Yet you drew me out of the womb;
> you entrusted me to my mother's breasts.
> You placed me on your lap from my birth,
> from my mother's womb you have been my God.
> Do not stand aside: trouble is near
> and I have no one to help me.

It is as though the psalmist speaks out one thought in detail and then waits for a response. During the silence another thought strikes him, and he voices that in some detail and again waits. It is possible that the progression of thoughts itself is God's response, or is elicited by that silent presence. Sometimes people who pray like this will say that although God was silent, he seemed to be listening attentively.

The psalmist now goes even deeper into a description of his misery.

> A herd of bulls surrounds me,
> strong bulls of Bashan close in on me.
> Their mouths are wide open for me,

> like lions tearing and roaring.
> I am like water draining away,
> my bones are all disjointed,
> and my heart is like wax,
> melting inside me.
> My throat is drier than baked clay
> and my tongue sticks to my mouth.
> A pack of dogs surrounds me;
> a gang of villains closes in on me.
> They tie me hand and foot
> and leave me dying in the dust of death.
> I can count every one of my bones;
> they glare and gloat over me.
> They divide my garments among them,
> and cast lots for my clothes.

Perhaps the silence of God allows us the space to spell out all of our pain and suffering. Often enough even with our closest friends we cannot say all that is in our troubled hearts because they cannot take the pain and have to interrupt with comforting words.

In the silence that follows that outburst the psalmist once again turns to God with a plea for help.

> Do not stand aside, Yahweh.
> O my strength, come quickly to my help;
> rescue my soul from the sword,
> my life from the grip of the dog.
> Save me from the lion's mouth,
> my poor soul from the wild bulls' horns!

One gets the impression that God seems closer than he did at the beginning of the prayer. The prayer is more tender, less stark and despairing.

Often people who continue to pour out their hearts to God

even when he seems far away notice such a change in their mood. If asked to reflect on what happened, they might say that after each silence God seemed to be closer, seemed to be listening, seemed to care. I believe that many fail to find such growing comfort because they are afraid to pour out all their feelings, even their resentment at the way God seems to treat them. The prophet Jeremiah is not so leery.

> I never sat in the company of revelers,
> never made merry with them;
> I sat alone because your hand was on me
> and you had filled me with indignation.
> Why is my pain unending
> and my wound grievous and incurable?
> Will you be to me like a deceptive brook,
> like a spring that fails? (Jer 15:17–18)

And he too felt a more consoling presence.

At this point the psalm takes the sudden turn toward praise that we mentioned earlier.

> Then I will proclaim your name,
> praise you in full assembly:
> "You who fear Yahweh, praise God!
> Entire race of Abraham and Sarah, glorify God!
> Entire race of Israel, revere God!
> For Yahweh has not despised
> or disdained the poor in their poverty,
> has not hidden from them,
> but has answered when they called."

The sufferer has been heard and he has felt the comfort of the God who at the beginning seemed so distant. Often this experience is repeated by people who persevere in pouring out their hearts to God. We can only hope that Jesus too experienced the closeness of Abba. Luke seems to indicate that such was the case. "Jesus called out with a loud voice, 'Father, into your hands I commit my spirit.' When he had said this, he breathed his last" (Lk 23:46).

The pattern I have described can be seen in other psalms (e.g., Pss 6, 12, and 13) and in other scenes of the bible. Recall that Hannah poured out her soul to the Lord and that when she went away her countenance was no longer sad. I can only encourage people who feel burdened by life's sorrows to try what has so often been a comforting way to pray.

Chapter VII

Feelings of Rage and Vengeance

Have you ever felt so angry at someone or at a situation that you really wanted to hurt others, even maim or kill? You may have been personally wronged or injured by another, but you may also have felt so angry when you read in the newspaper of a brutal attack on a frail, elderly woman or saw pictures of the corpses piled up at Auschwitz. The bile may be rising again in your throat as you remember some of these times. In moments like these we can be very vindictive, and if anyone tries to talk us into forgiveness, he/she soon feels the heat of our wrath. We probably do not spontaneously think of prayer in these moments either. Oh, we might turn to God to ask for a forgiving heart after we have calmed down, but in the heat of the moment such a prayer would be impossible. What we probably would find hard to believe is that we could actually tell God how angry we are and what we want to do to the victimizers. Yet this chapter will raise that possiblity as another way to develop our intimacy with God.

I have noticed that I tend to skip parts of the psalms because they seem so bloodthirsty. For example, when I ask people to pray together Psalm 139, I most often tell them to stop at the end of verse 18. Here is what follows in verses 19 to 22:

> God, if only you would destroy the wicked!
> They speak evil about you,
> regard your thoughts as nothing.
> Yahweh, I hate those who hate you
> and loathe those who rise against you.
> I hate them with a total hatred;
> they are my enemies, too.

I have noticed that others also avoid these lines when they pray this psalm publicly. We are embarrassed by the words and do not want to put them into our mouths.

Yet I do feel this vindictive at times. I have tried to take on the non-violent attitude of Jesus, but I know that at times I feel murderously angry. I am against capital punishment, for example; yet I can feel the gorge rise in me when I hear about sadistic rapes and torture and I want to see the perpetrators vindictively punished. "An eye for an eye" is the way I feel. I am embarrassed to admit such feelings, but they are real. And in the moments when I feel this way, if I were to pray what I feel, it would be in words like those I omit from Psalm 139. I suspect that I am not the only Christian of whom this is true. I want to invite reflection on this fact.

Suppose that you have just been grossly insulted by someone at work, and you are still seething when you meet your best friend. What would you do? Talk about the weather? Or the latest gossip? Or sports? If you did not say anything about your anger and resentment, your conversation would be rather bland and boring, would it not? After all, the only thing on your mind and heart is what happened to you at work. Why would you not speak of the incident to your friend? Probably you are afraid that you will lose control, will rant and rave, and make a fool of yourself. Or perhaps you are afraid that your friend will get so incensed at your enemy that he or she will want to help you to get revenge. Or perhaps you do not want to poison your friend's attitude toward the one who insulted you. Whatever the reason, if you do not reveal yourself at this time, you are holding back something of yourself from the relationship. And since your friend would have to be rather insensitive not to notice that something is wrong with you, your reticence may send a shadow over the relationship, at least for the moment.

I believe that the same reasoning can be used of our relationship with God. If in prayer we are unwilling to tell God how enraged we are at our co-worker, we will have nothing to say to him of any consequence. It may well be that we are bored in prayer because we do not want to say what is really in our hearts.

But how can we tell God that we want to kill our co-worker or strangle our spouse? Is that not a sin? I am reminded of a wonderful passage in Ana-Maria Rizzuto's *Birth of the Living God* where she says that the analyst's office "in fact offers the patient the opportunity to use the safety of its playful ground to display unspeakable intimate wishes toward people who should never know about them. . . . If we could not kiss those we should not kiss, if we could not hate those we should not hate . . . if we could not kill those who should remain alive . . . then life would be miserable indeed. We can entertain all these fantasies as play. . . ." When I read the passage, I immediately thought that it rang even truer of one's prayer room. To God one can say things that one would not, and perhaps should not, say to anyone. At the least we can assert that the writers of the psalms were not afraid to say some rather frightful things to God.

Once more the analogy to friendship may be helpful. If I

can tell my friend how enraged I am at my co-worker, I at least let off steam. That can save me from ulcers or high-blood pressure. If he/she is a good friend, what will happen? I will be listened to sympathetically. My friend may even feel angry at the co-worker as well, but probably not with the same murderous intensity I have. The late Rollin Fairbanks once told a story in a class on pastoral counseling. He was counseling a woman who was extremely angry at the abusive treatment she was receiving from her husband and her mother-in-law. As she expressed her anger, her rage grew even stronger. Rollin listened sympathetically, but he admitted that he began to get a little nervous when she talked of killing her mother-in-law. Then she blurted out that she would kill her, would stab her to death. Rollin then said that if she killed her she would have to go to the funeral. She yelled out, "I won't go! I won't!" and then she realized what she had said, caught some of Rollin's humor, started to cry, and said, "What am I going to do?" In other words, in this safe atmosphere she was enabled not only to vent her feelings, but also to become aware of how desperate she felt and then was able to ask for help. Before this she had just been feeling sorry for herself and had not been able to ask what she might do to change her situation. Once she saw that her present situation was leading her to murderous thoughts, she knew that she had to do something for herself.

For centuries Jews and Christians have prayed the psalms. Perhaps we have not often in that time adverted to the fact that the expression of personal rage could be an acceptable prayer and even an exercise of intimacy. Psalm 139 is one of the easier psalms to accept since the psalmist, after all, is only expressing hatred for God's enemies. There are others that are considerably more difficult. In Psalm 18, for instance, the warrior king exults in prayer at the carnage he has wreaked on his enemies with the help of God.

(The God) who trained my hands
so that my arms can bend a bronze bow.
You have given me the shield of your salvation;
your right hand supported me, and your help made me
    great.

.   .   .   .

I pursued my enemies and overtook them,
and did not turn back till they were crushed.
I left them shattered, not able to rise;
they fell under my feet. (Ps 18:34–38)

This man tells God exactly what he feels. Whether God
then led him gradually to more peaceful ways, we do not
know. We do know that such tutoring has taken place in
history. St. Ignatius, in his autobiography, tells us that early
in his conversion he could not make up his mind in prayer
whether to go after and kill a Moor who had seemed to
besmirch our Lady's name. He prayed much on the choice
but could not come to a conclusion. So he let his mule make
the choice for him by giving the mule free rein. Luckily for
the Moor and, perhaps, St. Ignatius, the mule did not take
the road the Moor took. Gradually God taught Ignatius how
to discern, and Ignatius gave up his sword forever.

Even more difficult to stomach is the ending of the beauti-
ful song of lament, Psalm 137.

By the rivers of Babylon
we sat and wept, remembering Zion.
On the poplars of that land
we hung up our harps;
There our captors asked of us
the lyrics of our songs
and urged us to be joyous:
"Sing for us one of the songs of Zion!" they said.
How could we sing a song of Yahweh
while in a foreign land?

If I forget you, Jerusalem,
may my right hand forget its skill!
May my tongue cleave to the roof of my mouth
if I forget you,
if I do not consider Jerusalem
my greatest joy
Remember, Yahweh, what the Edomites did
that day in Jerusalem.
When they said "Tear it down,
tear it down to its foundations!"
O daugher of Babylon—you destroyer—
happy those who repay you
the evil you have done us!
Happy those who shall seize and smash
your little ones against the rock! (Ps 137)

We find these last words hard to take. We want to wipe them out of the book of the Lord, to explain them away as the expression of a primitive people who did not know better. But we might better look to our hearts and recognize that such rage and vengeance is not far from us. And if we are kept from voicing such vengeful feelings, let us hope and pray that it is by the grace of God and not just because we are afraid to look or sound bad or to get hurt.

The point is that we can only be saved from our worst feelings by the grace of God. We cannot will away our feelings of rage or vengeance or lust. We can try to control their expression in behavior, of course. But to change the feelings themselves we need the grace of God. Indeed one way to obtain such grace is to pour out our feelings to God in all their rawness and savagery. As we do, we may well begin to feel the rage soften so that like Rollin Fairbanks' client we can then say, "Help me to figure out what to do with this situation that has caused me to feel like this."

Chapter VIII

On the Revelation of Sin

God, search me and know my heart;
probe me and know my thoughts.
Make sure I do not follow evil ways,
and guide me in the way of life eternal. (Ps. 139:23–24)

In the last chapter we noted a tendency in ourselves to block
out the vengeful feelings of verses 19 to 22 of Psalm 139. As
we read these last two verses of the psalm, we may feel a
similar interior squirming. Ask the living God to search me
and know my heart and to show me my wicked way—the
psalmist must be joking! Truth to tell, we will not say these
words and mean them if we do not believe in our bones that
God is on our side. Who would ask a snooping, vengeful God
to probe his/her heart? Only a masochist would dare. Yet
these verses reveal a profound theological truth, namely
that we cannot know our sinfulness without God's help,
without revelation. Only God can show us our sins; we
cannot show them to ourselves. In this chapter I want to
probe ways of letting God help us to know our evil ways.

A number of years ago I met a woman who could not open
the bible without experiencing condemnation. No matter
where she looked in the bible God seemed to be angry, blam-

ing, threatening punishment. So she gave up reading it since it made her so depressed. Quite obviously she had to miss seeing great gobs of the bible that depicted God as compassionate, caring, forgiving, loving. I presumed that her image of God kept her from noticing these parts of the bible and concluded that she needed a different experience of God to change her image of God. In the first and second chapters we discussed ways of having the foundational experience of being accepted by God, of feeling that one is the "apple of his eye" (Sebastian Moore). In terms of the Ignatian Spiritual Exercises we are speaking of an affective "First Principle and Foundation," an experience of one's basic identity as a person desired into existence by God. Before we have such a foundational experience, God is distant, fearsome, a snoop, and people often become scrupulous as they try to placate him. They need help to have a different experience of God, not exhortations or theological treatises that will only make them feel worse. This truth was the burden of the first and second chapters.

Once we really believe and experience that God did form our inmost being, did knit us together in our mothers' womb and we can praise him from our hearts (Ps 139:13–14), then we can ask him to reveal to us our evil ways. For then we will know experientially that God has our good at heart.

Of course, we will still make this prayer for the revelation of our sinfulness with fear and trepidation, just as we would tremble to ask our best friend to tell us honestly our faults and failings. We feel that we are not going to like what we see. And rightly so, because sin is precisely a blindness to our actual failings; hence when we ask someone we love to reveal to us our flaws, we open ourselves to a new view of ourselves. When the woman I mentioned earlier comes to believe in God's goodness to her from experience, she may also realize that her sinfulness consisted precisely in her poor self-image and her image of God as a bloodsucker and a tyrant, and not in the "sins" she regularly accused herself of. It really is revelation that we need and ask for when we say, and mean, the last words of Psalm 139. Hence, these words have to be based on trust in the goodness and kindness of God.

Such trust presupposed, how do we go about letting God reveal to us our sinfulness? First, we have to want him to do so. I suppose that such a desire only becomes real when we are already somewhat aware that something is awry in our relationship with him or with others. We become aware of a distance between us and God and wonder if we are causing it. At a workshop on prayer a role play brought out such an awareness. A woman described some very warm, close experiences of God which she had had two weeks before, but which had given way to periods of great dryness. As we looked carefully at her experience, she became aware that she was frightened as well as attracted by the closeness of God and had pulled back from God. She now had a motive to ask God to reveal what was making her so frightened of intimacy with him. In these circumstances she can recall the last time when she felt close to God and ask him to help to see what made her afraid. In her prayer she will begin to relive these moments of closeness and perhaps will again feel the fear arise, but now she will be alert to note what it is that brought it on.

People become aware of many sources of distance from a God who once seemed so close. They recall past sins and wonder if God has really forgiven them. They may have been hiding even from themselves a reality that makes them feel ashamed before God; for instance, many people who are concerned about their sexual identity feel such shame and do not like to be reminded of the issue. Likewise, while reading the gospels, they may come upon a text that raises a topic they had long suppressed. For example, a woman might read: "Therefore, if you are offering your gift at the altar and there remember that your brother has something against you, leave your gift there in front of the altar. First go and be reconciled with your brother; then come and offer your gift" (Mt 5:23–24). She suddenly recalls something her brother did to her years ago for which she has never forgiven him, and finds the gorge rise in her again. Or a man might hear this text read at Sunday Mass: "If you lend money to one of my people among you who is needy, do not be like a moneylender; charge him no interest" (Ex 22:25) and find himself thinking about his tenants in the inner city who are paying high rents for substandard housing. In these and many other ways God may be revealing our sinfulness to us. We are alerted to the possibility by noticing that the sense of closeness is missing again.

The last example reminds me of the story of Zacchaeus (Lk 19:1–10), the chief tax collector and a rich man. In one sense he made a big mistake. His curiosity got the better of him, and he climbed a sycamore tree to see who Jesus was. Jesus calls him down from the tree, "Zacchaeus, come down immediately. I must stay at your house today." Zacchaeus is delighted and receives the Lord into his house. Bystanders murmur that Jesus has gone in to eat with a sinner, but something happens to Zacchaeus just by being in the presence of Jesus. Seemingly without a word of censure from Jesus Zacchaeus stands and says, "Look, Lord! Here and now I give half of my possessions to the poor, and if I have cheated anybody out of anything, I will pay back four times the amount." Just being in the presence of God or of Jesus can remind us of our lack of holiness, our need for conversion.

Thus, if we try to stay close to God, or if we read or hear the bible attentively, we may find ourselves spontaneously reflecting on how we fail to treat others as God has treated us. Then the words of the Our Father will take new meaning: Forgive us our trespasses as we forgive those who have trespassed against us.

Another way to ask the Lord to reveal to us our sins is suggested by a contemplative reading of the cure of Bartimaeus, the blind beggar (Mk 10:46–52). Like Bartimaeus, we too often feel poor and blind and in need. Like him, we can cry out, "Jesus, Son of David, have mercy on me!" Bystanders rebuke Bartimaeus, telling him to be silent. We may hear inner voices that tell us to be silent. "Jesus would not have time for the likes of me." "I should be able to know my own sins; after all I know the commandments." "It's silly to think that Jesus will speak to me; it's all imagination." But Bartimaeus does not pay any attention to the rebukes; he shouts all the louder, "Son of David, have mercy on me!" Jesus calls him over, and Bartimaeus throws off his mantle, springs up and comes to Jesus. Jesus asks him: "What do you want me to do for you?" Imagine what might go through Bartimaeus as he hears these words. He is hopeful, delighted, eager. But does he have any doubts or fears? Does he wonder if his hopes will be raised only to be dashed when Jesus says that he cannot help him? As he thinks of asking to see, does he fear the changes that will come into his life if he gets his request? After all, the only livelihood he knows is begging and the only way he knows of coping with the world is as a blind man. So too, as we hear Jesus' words addressed to us, we may both tremble with excitement and hope and shake with fear. What will we see when Jesus opens our eyes to our sinfulness?

We know what Bartimaeus answers: "Rabbi, I want to see." What a great act of trust, to say so boldly that he wants his whole life changed. And Jesus says to him: "Go, your faith has healed you." The first sight Bartimaeus has is the face of Jesus, looking at him with love and, I believe, admiration. At least, that is one way of reading Jesus' words about the faith of Bartimaeus. The experience of the centuries since the time of Jesus tells us that those who ask Jesus to heal their blindness so that they can see their sinfulness and repent also look into the eyes of a lover, not an enemy.

The novelist J. R. R. Tolkien, in *The Fellowship of the Ring*, describes a meeting of eyes that captures what such a look might be like. The dwarf, Gimli, came with the rest of the fellowship into the land of Lothlorien, an elf kingdom. Dwarfs and elves have been traditional enemies, and suspicion has dogged this meeting. Galadriel, the queen of the elves, spoke in the language of the dwarfs.

> She looked upon Gimli, who sat glowering and sad, and she smiled. And the Dwarf, hearing the names given in his own ancient tongue, looked up and met her eyes; and it seemed to him that he looked suddenly into the heart of an enemy and saw there love and understanding. Wonder came into his face, and then he smiled in answer. (p. 461)

Many Christians have looked into the eyes of Jesus and where they had expected to see condemnation they have seen love.

Chapter IX

The Forgiveness of Sin

It is one thing to ask God to reveal my sins, another to ask him to forgive them. Of course, the very act of revealing my sins may be experienced as forgiveness, but often enough we need to ask to know explicitly that we are forgiven. In this chapter I want to look at ways of turning to the Lord for such forgiveness.

First, we need to notice what forgiveness entails. If we have hurt a friend would we be satisfied if the friend merely forgoes retaliation? In fact, it shows great forbearance and kindness if our friend does not retaliate tit-for-tat. But we want more, don't we? We want a restoration of the friendship. We want the return of intimacy. We promise our friend that we will not hurt him/her in that way again because we want to be trusted again. In a sense we are asking our hurt friend to take another chance on us, to let us back into the very closeness that made it possible for us to hurt him/her in the first place. With God we may also be motivated by the fear of punishment, the fear of hell; but even then we are also motivated by the desire for the return of closeness, by love.

Again the story of God's dealings with the Israelites in the desert, in spite of much of the gore and killing, may be

instructive to us. In the book of Exodus, chapter 24, God
invites Moses to the mountain to hear and receive the law
and commandments. In chapters 24 to 31 Moses listens to
God's commands. In the meantime the people get restless
and demand that Aaron make them gods of gold. Moses
returns with the tablets of the commandments and finds the
people making merry and adoring the golden calf. Moses
calls to his side those who will stand with Yahweh and
instructs them to kill all who still worship the false god.
Three thousand die. In chapter 33 Yahweh tells Moses:
"Leave this place, you and the people you brought up out of
Egypt, and go up to the land I promised on oath to Abraham,
Isaac, and Jacob, saying, 'I will give it to your descendants.' . . . Go up to the land flowing with milk and honey.
But I will not go with you, because you are a stiff-necked
people and I might destroy you on the way" (Ex 33:1–3).
Notice that the people are not deprived of the promised
land; the only deprivation threatened is that God will not go
with them. "When the people heard these distressing words,
they began to mourn and no one put on any ornaments" (v.
4). It would seem that they want the restoration of intimacy
with God. And when God does relent and does promise to go
with them, they have the opportunity to betray God again.
That is the risk God takes when he forgives from the heart.

One approach to asking such a restoration of friendship is
given us in Psalm 51.

> In your goodness, O God, have mercy on me;
> with gentleness wipe away my faults.
> Cleanse me of my guilt;
> free me from my sins.

Here the psalmist reminds God of the name he revealed to
Moses, recorded in Ex 34:6: "The Lord, the Lord, the compassionate and gracious God, slow to anger, abounding in love

and faithfulness . . ." The psalmist relies on God's self-
revelation because he knows that he cannot earn forgiveness.

> My faults are always before me;
> my sins haunt my mind.
> I have sinned against you and no other—
> knowing that my actions were wrong in your eyes.
> Your judgment is what I deserve;
> your sentence extremely fair.

When we come before God as sinners, we can enumerate the
ways we have offended him. It may seem strange to tell God
our sins. After all God is the one who has revealed them to
us. Surely he does not have to be reminded of what we have
done or omitted. The recital, however, is not for his sake,
but for ours. When we detail our sins, we are saying in
effect: "Do you forgive me for this, and this, and this . . . ?"
Often enough the unspoken offense to a friend, the one we
have not thought of or have been afraid to ask forgiveness
for, comes back later to haunt us. "Is my friend still harbor-
ing that grudge?" The same dynamic can trouble even more
our relationship with the Lord.

And what do we want of God? The psalmist again puts
words in our mouths.

> But you love true sincerity,
> so you teach me the paths of wisdom.
> Until I am clean, bathe me with hyssop;
> wash me until I am whiter than snow.
> Infuse me with joy and gladness;
> let these bones you have crushed dance for joy.
> Please do not stare at my sins;
> blot out all my guilt.

We want a full pardon, a clean bill of health, an assurance
that our sins will not stand in the way of friendship. For the
psalmist goes on:

> Create a pure heart in me, O my God,
> renew me with a steadfast spirit.
> Don't drive me away from your presence,
> or take your Holy Spirit from me.
> Once more be my savior; revive my joy.
> Strengthen and sharpen my still weak spirit.

We want a restoration of intimacy and friendship. Our joy
does not consist in slavish obedience to God's commands,
but in being one with God, in knowing again that we are the
apple of his eye. Indeed the psalmist goes on to speak of
working together with God to bring other transgressors back
to God's ways and to lead the restored people in praise. The
restoration of intimacy leads to collaboration.

The gospels provide a number of contemplative possibilities for approaching Jesus for forgiveness. The healing mira-
cles are one example. However, I want to take up two
passages that feature Peter since both of them have proven
helpful to many Christians. The first is the scene of the
washing of the feet in John 13. The chapter opens very
solemnly.

> It was just before the Passover Feast. Jesus knew that the
> time had come for him to leave this world and go to the
> Father. Having loved his own who were in the world, he
> now showed them the full extent of his love. The evening
> meal was being served, and the devil had already prompted
> Judas Iscariot, the son of Simon, to betray Jesus. Jesus
> knew that the Father had put all things under his power,
> and that he had come from God and was returning to God;
> so he got up from the meal, took off his outer clothing, and

> wrapped a towel around his waist. After that, he poured
> water into a basin and began to wash his disciples' feet,
> drying them with the towel that was wrapped around him.
> (Jn 13:1–5)

Those who are aware that Jesus knows exactly what kind
of persons they are, how they have betrayed the values of
Jesus and over and over again failed to live up to their own
best selves, can feel solidarity with the disciples at this moment. The disciples are so unsure of their integrity that
moments later they will wonder which of them is the be-
trayer. In the synoptics we read that they even ask: "Is it I,
Lord?" The evangelist underlines the knowledge of Jesus at
this moment. As we contemplate this scene, we can feel in
our bones that he knows each one of us thoroughly.

Many people who thus contemplate this passage feel the
same reluctance voiced by Peter. They feel unworthy and
find it very difficult to let Jesus wash their feet. "You shall
never wash my feet," says the Peter in each of us. We find it
extremely hard to accept undeserved service and forgiveness
and love from anyone, and especially Jesus. For we cannot
do anything to earn his love; worse yet, we know how often
we betray him and what he stands for. And he tells us what
he is about:

> Do you understand what I have done for you? You call me
> "Teacher" and "Lord," and rightly so, for that is what I
> am. Now that I, your Lord and Teacher, have washed your
> feet, you also should wash one another's feet. I have set
> you an example that you should do as I have done for you.
> (vv. 12–15)

Perhaps part of our reluctance to accept his forgiveness derives from the realization that we will then be called to give
up our own grudges. But the deepest level of reluctance

comes, it seems, from the difficulty of accepting an absolutely free gift. But when we do accept it, we can experience the effusion of Peter: "Then, Lord, not just my feet but my hands and my head as well!"

In this scene of the last supper we also see the consequences for Jesus of receiving Peter and the other disciples back into intimacy. They can fail him again. Judas actually does follow through on his betrayal, Peter denies knowledge of his friend three times, and all run away and leave him. It is as though Jesus throws his arms around the sinner in forgiveness only to find that the one restored thus to intimacy can again stab him in the back. And this leads us to the scene in John 21 where Peter meets the risen Lord whom he has denied.

The chapter opens with the scene of the miraculous catch of fish. When John tells Peter that it is the Lord on shore, Peter cannot wait to land. He puts on his clothes and jumps into the sea. Then the following scene takes place.

> When they had finished eating, Jesus said to Simon Peter, "Simon son of John, do you truly love me more than these?" "Yes, Lord," he said, "you know that I love you." Jesus said, "Feed my lambs." Again Jesus said, "Simon son of John, do you truly love me?" He answered, "Yes, Lord, you know that I love you." Jesus said, "Take care of my sheep." The third time he said to him, "Simon son of John, do you love me?" Peter was hurt because Jesus asked him the third time, "Do you love me?" He said, "Lord, you know all things; you know that I love you." Jesus said, "Feed my sheep." (Jn 21:15–17)

Jesus is experienced as very tender and caring in this scene. Instead of a tongue lashing Peter is given the chance to atone for the triple denial with a triple affirmation of his love for Jesus. And note that Peter says to Jesus, "You know all things." The text seems to say that Peter is able to affirm his love for Jesus even though he knows that Jesus knows him inside out, knows all his flaws and weaknesses. People who use this text for prayer and put themselves in the shoes of Peter experience Jesus as overpoweringly forgiving. Moreover, Jesus not only forgives Peter, but also asks him to take care of Jesus' flock. Peter is brought back into intimacy with interest to spare. Jesus not only trusts him with his own heart again, but also entrusts to him his beloved people. Here forgiveness and the invitation to collaboration in the apostolate are united.

In his *Spiritual Exercises* Ignatius invites the retreatant who has meditated on his sins to speak familiarly with Jesus on the cross. When people do this, they often find it hard at first to look Jesus directly in the eyes. But when they do, they see the eyes of forgiving love. Ignatius then suggests that the retreatant mull over the questions: What have I done for Christ? What am I doing for Christ? What will I do for Christ? This kind of colloquy comes easily to one who has experienced the kind of forgiveness Peter experienced beside the Sea of Tiberias.

Chapter X

Expressing Gratitude

When we have poured out our hearts and been heard, when we have asked for forgiveness and felt that it has been offered to us, gratitude wells up in our hearts, and we want to thank God. It may be a help to look at different ways of saying thanks to God.

We can begin with Psalm 107:

> Alleluia!
> Give thanks to Yahweh who is good;
> whose love endures forever.
> Let these be the words of Yahweh's redeemed,
> those redeemed from the hands of the foe
> by gathering them home from foreign lands,
> from east and west, from north and south.
> Some had strayed in the wilderness and the desert,
> not finding a way to an inhabited town.
> Hungry and thirsty,
> their life was wasting away.
> Then they cried to Yahweh in their anguish,
> and Yahweh rescued them from their distress,
> Guiding them by a straight road
> to a city where they could live.

Let them thank Yahweh for his faithful love,
for these deeds on our behalf.
Satisfying the hungry,
Yahweh fills the hungry with good things. (Ps 107:1–9)

The psalm goes on in this vein. It reminds different groups
of people of the plight they were in when they cried to the
Lord and he rescued them. Then they are urged to give
thanks to the Lord for his unfailing love. Thus, one way that
we give thanks is by remembering the gracious deeds of the
Lord. Indeed it is when we forget what God has done for us
that we begin to look down on others, to take pride in our
own accomplishments, and thus fall into sin. This is the
burden of the parable of the unmerciful servant in Matthew
18:22–35. The unmerciful servant receives forgiveness of
his enormous debt when he begs the king for mercy. But he
immediately forgets what has been done to him and puts
into debtors' prison a fellow servant who owes him a pit-
tance. So ingratitude leads to moral blindness, hardness of
heart and lack of compassion; gratitude will keep us humble, compassionate, able to see things as they really are.

Here we might remind ourselves of the root meaning of
Eucharist. It comes from the Greek meaning thanksgiving.
In the Eucharist we remind ourselves of all the saving deeds
of God toward us as a people and as individuals and we give
thanks.

The psalm and the Eucharist also indicate that prayers of
thanksgiving can be inexhaustible. We never need to run
out of conversation material with the Lord. Our whole life is
a gift, and we can, therefore, continually discover more
things for which to thank God. The wonders of creation, for
example, are inexhaustible and the work of God's hands. We
can thank God for everything we see, touch, hear, smell that
gives us pleasure. To get a little idea of how endless such a

prayer of thanksgiving can be, read the canticle of the three young men in Daniel 3:51–90. "Light and darkness, bless the Lord! Lightnings and clouds, bless the Lord! Birds of the air, bless the Lord! etc., etc."

Another way to develop the prayer of gratitude is to spend time in prayer asking God to help us to see our lives as our personal salvation history. In the book, *God and You,* I indicated that one can ask God for such help and then recall an image from childhood, for example, the family home or some loved one, and let the memories rise almost as a free association. In such a way we could go through all the periods of our lives in order to discover how God has been present to us and saving and helping us in all the vicissitudes of life. We might be led to write our own psalm of thanksgiving by listing the various saving events of our lives.

Not that we will experience every memory as positive and pleasant. In fact, some memories may bring back feelings of resentment and anger at people in our past and at God who did not seem to care when we were in pain. If this happens, then we can tell God how we felt and feel, as we noted earlier. "Where were you when my father beat my mother and us?" "What kind of salvation history did you put me in when . . . ?" Strangely enough this kind of prayer can lead to acceptance and gratitude—though it may take some time.

Bartimaeus, the blind beggar of Mark 10, must have accepted his past. He is a blind man, a blind beggar. He does not seem to wallow in resentment at what life has done to him; if he did, he would not have been able to ask so forcibly for his sight. To come to this point of acceptance he may have had to go through all the stages of grief described so well by Elisabeth Kübler-Ross. He may have denied his blindness, raged at it, at life, and at God, bargained with God, and become depressed. But now he has accepted that he is blind. And yet it is accepted as somehow *past,* as not controlling his freedom *now*, his freedom to desire a change. "Rabbi, I want to see."

It is important to grasp the full impact of what it means for Bartimaeus, or anyone of us, to accept the past. It does not mean a stoic impassivity toward life. It does not mean a rosy optimism either. Life has dealt Bartimaeus a cruel blow, as it has dealt cruel blows to many people. Children have been subjected to abusive, unloving and unskilled parenting and have been physically, psychically and spiritually scarred as a result. Loved ones have tragically and permanently been parted, and the survivors are wounded deeply. To accept the past does not mean to condone everyone and everything. But it does mean to forgive in some deep way.

Søren Kierkegaard makes a powerful statement in *Fear and Trembling* while commenting on the biblical story of Tobias and Sarah. Recall that Sarah has become a mockery to her own maid because seven men have married her and died on their marriage night. Now Tobias has asked to marry her. Many see Tobias as the hero. "No," says Kierkegaard,

> it is Sarah that is the heroine. . . . For what love of God it requires to be willing to let oneself be healed when from the beginning one has been thus bungled without one's fault, from the beginning one has been an abortive specimen of humanity! What ethical maturity was required for assuming the responsibility of allowing the loved one to do such a daring deed! What humility before the face of another person! What faith in God to believe that the next instant she would not hate the husband to whom she owed everything!

To accept the past as *my* past brings a freedom from it. But freedom does not mean that I am no longer the person that past has made me. Bartimaeus is who he is because he has been a blind beggar. So too, Sarah is who she is because of her history of marriages.

Another example is supplied by a response of a young man who was born a hemophiliac; at any moment of his life he could bleed to death from a simple cut. He was asked whether he wished that he had not had the illness. "How can I—or anyone—wish that the most important thing that ever happened to me had not happened? It is like saying that I wish I had been born on another planet, so different would I probably be. Put it this way: I would not have it any other way."

And yet with this acceptance there also comes a freedom from the past. Bartimaeus is free of the imprisoning identity: "blind beggar." Even if he does not receive his sight, he is free to become blind Bartimaeus the poet, or blind Bartimaeus the husband of Mary, or blind Bartimaeus the follower of Jesus. So too the young hemophiliac can, by accepting his past, become a doctor, a teacher, a husband who also happens to be hemophiliac. To accept the past as my past means to accept a future limited by *my* past, but nonetheless a future.

Erik Erikson calls his final developmental stage the crisis between ego integrity and despair. Ego integrity or wisdom is described in *Childhood and Society:* "It is the acceptance of one's one and only life cycle as something that had to be and that, by necessity, permitted of no substitutions: it thus means a new, a different love of one's parents." This is what I meant earlier when I said that such acceptance means to forgive at a deep level. Such acceptance is not an achievement of our wills, but a grace for which we beg in prayer. And the result is gratitude. Listen to these words of Robert Massie, Jr., the young hemophiliac, and see if you can sense the gratitude he has.

Am I rationalizing? . . . To say that would be to say that I
have come through the pain and troubles of my first eigh-
teen years with nothing to show for it. To believe that
would be to believe that I learned nothing of human nature
and kindness through all the years of hospitals, that my
parents were unable to impart more than an average sense
of faith through all my setbacks. If this were true, if having
vanquished braces, bleeding, pain, self-consciousness, bore-
dom, and depression, I have not added in any way to my
appreciation of this life that has been given me, then that
indeed would be a misfortune to be pitied. (Robert Massie
and Suzanne Massie, *Journey*. New York: Knopf, 1975, p.
360)

It is a great grace to thank God even for what seem to be
tragedies in life. Make no mistake. I am not exhorting readers to such gratitude. Rather, like Dylan Thomas to his dying father, I would exhort those who feel anger and resentment at life's hurts to "rage, rage against the dying of the
light." And, of course, also to ask God to be present, to help
us to believe that the night is "good." Then, perhaps, we too
will experience God's saving help and be able to pray with
all our hearts:

Then they cried to Yahweh in the anguish
who rescued them from their distress.
God sent a word to heal them
and saved them from the grave.
Let them thank Yahweh for this unfailing love,
for these wonderful deeds on our behalf.
Let them offer thanksgiving sacrifices
and sing with joy what Yahweh has done. (Ps 107:19–22)

Chapter XI

Making Our Own Psalm of Gratitude

In the last chapter I indicated that we might want to make up our own psalm of gratitude to God. I want to use part of the infancy narrative in Luke's gospel to point the way.

In the first chapter of Luke we meet an old, childless couple, Zechariah and Elizabeth, and Elizabeth's cousin, a young slip of a girl named Mary. Their stories have resonances with the story of Hannah, the mother of Samuel, whom we met in the fifth chapter, and with the story of Abraham and Sarah, whom we met in the third chapter. Like Sarah, Elizabeth is barren. Like Abraham, Zechariah hears a promise of a son and is incredulous. Mary's Magnificat bears striking resemblances to Hannah's song of thanksgiving when she brings Samuel to the temple. Chapter 1 of Luke tingles with the excitement of the extraordinary and mysterious, with the joy which the closeness of God brings. I invite the reader to reflect contemplatively with me.

Verses 5 to 7 establish who Zechariah and Elizabeth are, ending with the poignant line: "But they had no children, because Elizabeth was barren; and they were both well along in years." On this sad note Zechariah enters by lot

into the holy of holies of the temple where he is startled by a
vision. The nearness of God often arouses fear in us humans. But the angel has good news, not bad for Zechariah.
His barren wife will bear a son who "will be a joy and delight to you, and many will rejoice because of his birth."
Zechariah, like many of us, cannot believe the good news.
"How can I be sure of this?" When he comes out, he is mute
and can only make signs that something extraordinary has
happened to him. And the impossible comes to pass; Elizabeth becomes pregnant. God has removed her "disgrace" as
he had done for Hannah.

The scene now shifts to Nazareth where a virgin receives
an even more incredible visitation of God's emissary. Again
we note the fear aroused by the sensed nearness of God, and
once again good news is announced. Given the implications
of the announcement and of the invitation for all subse-
quent history it seems like an understatement to call it good
news. One can almost sense the universe hold its breath as
the angel awaits Mary's answer. Think of what is riding on
her reply! One experiences a sigh of relief and wonder as
Mary says: "I am the Lord's servant. . . . May it be to me as
you have said." She may be just a slip of a girl, but with her
answer, one might say, the world pivoted in a new direction.
No wonder Christians want to bow their heads or bend their
knees, for here, in this tiny hamlet of a backwater, captive
nation, with the acceptance of a young girl, "the Word became flesh and made his dwelling among us" (Jn 1:14).

After this scene Mary hurries to visit Elizabeth. As she
greets Elizabeth, the baby in Elizabeth's womb leaps for joy,
and Elizabeth says to Mary what Christians down through
the ages have wanted to say to her for what she did for us:
"Blessed are you among women and blessed is the child you
will bear. But why am I so favored, that the mother of my
Lord should come to me? As soon as the sound of your

greeting reached my ears, the baby in my womb leaped for joy. Blessed is she who has believed that what the Lord has said to her will be accomplished!" God has come as close as he possibly can, and the response is not, finally, fear and trembling, but unbounded joy. John leaping in the womb for joy reminds us of all those other instances in the bible where God's presence brings incredible joy and sets the feet dancing and the voice singing. Recall the song of Moses and Miriam after God saved the Israelites from the army of the pharaoh at the Red Sea (Ex 15:1–21) or David dancing "with all his might" before the ark as it is brought into Jerusalem (1 Sam 6:14–15) or Psalm 149, "Let them praise God's name in a festive dance; let them sing praise to God with timbrel and harp" (3). My favorite such image occurs in Acts 3 when the crippled beggar is cured. "He jumped to his feet and began to walk. Then he went with them into the temple courts, walking and jumping, and praising God" (8).

What just happened as I wrote the last paragraph may give us a clue about how to write our own psalm of gratitude. When I started, I had no idea that I would be reminded of the images of dancing for joy. They came by association as I pondered the words of the Lukan text. If we let ourselves feel the emotions aroused by contemplation of the scriptural texts, we will find ourselves spontaneously flying from image to image as our hearts and minds try to express all that is aroused in us by the sense of God's presence and goodness and kindness.

In the text of Luke's first chapter Mary now breaks out into song, her Magnificat, as it is called from the first word of the song in the Latin translation. The author has put into Mary's mouth a song that is like a patchwork quilt of references to Old Testament texts. The associative process seems to have taken over his writing hand. With the help of the Jerusalem Bible's translation and side references I want to show the results of this creative associative process. The translation highlights phrases taken from the Old Testament.

> My soul proclaims the greatness of the Lord
> and my spirit *exults in God my saviour;* (1 Sam 2:1;
>   Hab 3:18)
> because *he has looked upon his lowly handmaid.* (1 Sam
>   1:11)
> Yes, from this day forward all generations will call me
>   blessed,
> for the Almighty has done great things for me.
> *Holy is his name,* (Ps 111:9)
> and *his mercy reaches from age to age*
> *for those who fear him.* (Ps 103:17)
> He has shown the power of his arm,
> he has routed the proud of heart.
> *He has pulled down the princes* from their thrones (Job
>   12:19)
> *and exalted the lowly.* (Job 5:11)
> *The hungry he has filled with good things,* (Ps 107:9)
> the rich sent empty away.
> *He has come to the help of Israel his servant,* (Is 41:8–9)
> *mindful of his mercy* (Ps 98:3)
> —according to the promise he made to our ancestors—
> of his mercy to Abraham and to his descendants for
>   ever.

The author has remembered phrases from various parts of the bible which bear on the theme of Mary's joy and thanksgiving. Mary's situation of being miraculously pregnant recalls Hannah's story and her song of thanksgiving. Mary is just a young girl (a lowly handmaid) whom God has exalted. God has not chosen the strong and powerful, but the weak and humble. We are reminded of Paul's statement: "But God chose the foolish things of the world to shame the wise;

God chose the weak things of the world to shame the strong. He chose the lowly things of this world and despised things—and the things that are not—to nullify the things that are, so that no one may boast before him" (1 Cor 1:27–29). Contemplation of the mystery of Mary reminds the author of Luke of sayings from the psalms and Job and Isaiah that echo the same theme. Besides the highlighted phrases, which are almost direct quotes, there are many other references to biblical themes in the text. The song is a patchwork quilt.

If we want to write our own psalm of gratitude and praise of God, we can take a leaf from Luke. We can begin with our own thoughts and feelings and let them move as they will. We may be reminded of poems or lines or phrases that hit off what we want to say. Biblical words and images may spring to mind. Jot them all down. You may want to look up the texts or you may not. Note that the author of Luke seems to work from memory. The point is not to attain the accuracy of the scholar, but to try to tell God how grateful we are with as much creativity and fullness as we can manage. After we have let the associations and memories come, then we can try our hand at putting together a psalm, stitching in as many of the themes and phrases as we can. No one else has to read our psalm unless we want to share it as the psalmists did. Just trying such an exercise in the privacy of our own room or in a chapel can be a freeing and joyful experience and open new ways to relate to God. Like the juggler of Notre Dame we do our thing without witnesses before God, and "your Father, who sees what is done in secret, will reward you" (Mt 6:6).

Chapter XII

Getting To Know Jesus

In the course of these chapters on intimacy with God we have stressed the value of transparency, of letting God know what we actually think and feel, even when we do not like or are horrified by what we think and feel. We have also indicated that the relationship with God is a mutual one, that God reveals his thoughts and feelings, what he values, how he reacts to us. In prayer we have learned a great deal about God as well as about ourselves. The desire to "know" God, "know" in the Johannine sense of "know-love," sits deep within our hearts, even if, as we have noted, the desire is often muted by our fear of God and of ourselves. As Christians we believe that Jesus of Nazareth is the Incarnation, the "flesh-taking" as Rosemary Haughton translates it, of God, or, to be more correct, of God's Word or Son. If we would know-love God, our best bet is to know-love Jesus. The royal road to union with God runs through Jesus of Nazareth. In the next few chapters I want to discuss how we get to know-love Jesus.

I invite you to contemplate a scene in the first chapter of John's gospel. John the Baptist has asserted that he is not the Christ, that he is the herald of the Christ. The next day he saw Jesus coming toward him and pointed to him as the

Lamb of God and gave testimony about him. Then follows
this scene:

> The next day John was there again with two of his disci-
> ples. When he say Jesus passing by, he said, "Look, the
> Lamb of God!" When the two disciples heard him say this,
> they followed Jesus. Turning around, Jesus saw them fol-
> lowing and asked, "What do you want?" They said, "Rab-
> bi" (which means Teacher), "where are you staying?"
> "Come," he replied, "and you will see." So they went and
> saw where he was staying, and spent that day with him. It
> was about the tenth hour. (Jn 1:35–39)

Can you put yourself into the shoes of these two disciples? You are invited to be with Jesus, and you are walking
after him. He turns to you and asks, "What do you want?"
What do you say to him? Remember that honesty is the best
policy. You may not want anything but to tag along at a
distance. You may want to know that you are forgiven. You
may want him to comfort you. Just ask him for what you
want. Relationships often founder when one or both parties
do not know what they want of each other. If I want a
shoulder to cry on, but do not tell you what I want, you may
misunderstand my inarticulateness as estrangement from
you and feel hurt. Or I may feel that you are cold-hearted
when you tell me about your day whereas you have no idea
that I need sympathy. In fact, I may not even know that I
want to cry on your shoulder until I articulate the desire. So
too, in our relationship with Jesus we need to return to this
scene again and again to hear Jesus ask us what we want.

In earlier chapters we have indicated ways of allowing
God or Jesus to give us what we want. We spoke of the
desire of overcoming our fears, for comfort, for healing, for
forgiveness. Now I want to assume that with the two disciples we too want to see where Jesus is staying. I take this

desire to mean that the disciples want to know more about
Jesus, that they want to spend time with him because they
are attracted to him. St. Ignatius, in what he calls the Second Week of the *Spiritual Exercises*, encourages the retreatant to ask for the grace to know Jesus better in order to
love him more deeply and to follow him more closely. The
musical *Godspell* put the same desire this way: "to see thee
more clearly, to love thee more dearly, to follow thee more
nearly." In effect, the disciples, and we who have such desires, want friendship with Jesus.

At first blush such a desire may be mind-boggling. When
we feel attracted to any human person, we feel somewhat
afraid, do we not? Afraid that we will not be found good
enough, interesting enough to this attractive person. Of
course, as Sebastian Moore rightly maintains in *Let This
Mind Be In You*, we would never desire to know-love anyone else if, at some level, we did not feel that we ourselves
were desirable. Still, we often abort our desire for friendship
or intimacy with another because of fear that the other will
not reciprocate the desire. Such a fear may be even stronger
when we feel the desire to know Jesus. What would help us
to get over this fear? In earlier chapters we have indicated
that experience is the only answer. If we have looked into
the eyes of Jesus and found there compassion and love, forgiveness and warmth, then such experiences whet our desire to know Jesus better and assure us that Jesus wants to
have us as his friends. The desire is aroused, for example,
when we can identify with Peter in John 21 and sense that
Jesus invites us to companionship with him or when we can
hear as addressed to us these words in John's account of the
last supper:

> Greater love has no one than this, that he lay down his life
> for his friends. You are my friends if you do what I com-

mand. I no longer call you servants, because a servant does not know his master's business. Instead, I have called you friends, for everything that I learned from my Father I have made known to you. You did not choose me, but I chose you and appointed you to go and bear fruit—fruit that will last. Then the Father will give you whatever you ask in my name. This is my command: Love each other. (Jn 15:13–17)

Let us presume that we have this desire to know-love Jesus. What is it that we want? We want to develop a friendship. But how do we develop any friendship? You do not do it by talking all the time. You do not do it by thinking about him or her a lot; that's a phantasy relationship. You do not do it when you are absorbed in yourself. You do it by trying to spend time with the other and by asking the other to tell you about him/herself. That means looking and listening, i.e., contemplating.

When we look and listen to the other, what do we want to know? We want to know the other's heart, his or her likes and dislikes, loves and hates, joys and sadness, don't we? Try to imagine a relationship without any heart. It would be a relationship with a computer robot. In fiction and movies even robots are given some affectivity, some heart, otherwise they would be dull and boring. Of course, you want some information about this person whom you want to get to know better. You would like to know where the person is from, how many brothers and sisters the person has, what schools he or she went to, etc. But would you be satisfied with that? What else would you like to know? You would want to know how the person felt about his or her family, birthplace, schools. You want to know the heart: the moods, the passions, the likes and dislikes, the values of the person. And ultimately you want to know how the person feels about you. So too, we want to know what and who Jesus cares about, values, loves, and hates. Nor does Jesus merely reveal information. He weeps over Jerusalem and calls the Pharisees whitened sepulchres. He yells at Peter in anger: "Get behind me, Satan!" So the first thing to be said about our contemplation of Jesus is that each of us desires to know his heart. Do you love me? Do you forgive me? Do you care for me the way you cared for Israel? Do you delight in what I delight in? What do you value? What are you like, Jesus? Tell me how you felt in the garden or when you washed the feet of the disciples. In every exercise of the *Spiritual Exercises* Ignatius has the exercitant ask for what he or she wants, and in all cases the desire is for self-revelation on the part of God or of Jesus in terms of the heart.

Once we see that this is what contemplation intends, we also see that it immediately involves our own heart. Friendships are mutual and require dialogue. Already my desire to know him is affective and may be deeply felt—so much so that I can become desolate if I do not get what I want, and like St. Teresa of Avila tell him off. At one point in her life she said to God, "if this is how you treat your friends, no wonder you have so few." What boggles the mind is the realization that Jesus wants to know me and wants me to know him.

This leads once again to the notion of transparency. Revelation of self does not come all at once. In fact, we may be afraid to ask Jesus to reveal himself totally, and may have to tell him to take it slowly. But note that revelation of self means to let oneself become more and more transparent before the other, and this can become scary. We may not like some of the affects that arise in us as we relate to Jesus nor some of his affective responses, either. However, as is true of all relationships, our relationship with Jesus will deepen as the two of us become more and more transparent before the other—in other words, when we are willing to see

Jesus as he really is and let him see us as we really are. Our friendship with him will stagnate when certain strong affects are consciously hidden from him or when we try to avoid strong feelings from him.

Here is one way to approach getting to know Jesus better. I begin by making known my desire to know him better, so that I may love him more and follow him more closely. Then I sit down and read the first ten chapters of Mark's gospel, if possible at one sitting. I let the gospel stories affect me, touch my imagination, rouse my emotions, set me thinking and desiring. The gospels are not dry historical tomes nor theological manuals. They are imaginative literature written to arouse the faith, hope and love of the readers. The gospel of Mark is considered the first written gospel, and it is packed with action and stories. So it is a good place to start to get to know Jesus better.

After I have finished reading the first ten chapters, I can reflect for a short time on what struck me about Jesus. How did I react to him? Did I like him? What stands out in memory? These first impressions are important because they tell me how Jesus is coming across to me now and perhaps what I need to talk to him about now. Sometimes people notice how hurried the pace is, how intense Jesus is. Sometimes we notice that he often took time off to pray to his Father, especially at important times in his life. Sometimes we are impressed with his compassion, and at other times we are caught up in his anger and ferocity and how he responds to the anger and violence of others. Sometimes we are attracted by his relationship with the apostles. Sometimes we are put off by his brusqueness. In prayer it will be helpful to return to whatever strikes us most forcibly in that first reading asking Jesus to deepen our knowledge and love of him or to help us to understand aspects of him that we did not like.

When we read the gospel in this way with the desire to

know Jesus better, we trust that he will take the occasion of our contemplation to reveal that aspect of himself which we need to and can grasp at this time. In other words, we trust that in contemplating the gospel we are also opening ourselves to a real encounter with the living Jesus who still wants companions at least as much as he did in his public life. We also trust that his Holy Spirit will use our contemplation and our imagination to reveal Jesus himself to us.

Ignatius of Loyola encourages retreatants to use their imaginations when they contemplate the gospels, to see the people in the scene, to hear what they are saying, smell the odors, etc. He even advises the retreatant to act as a servant to the Holy Family in the Nativity scene. So we need not be afraid to let our imaginations go, trusting that the Spirit will guide us.

Perhaps some of the following questions will help the reader to try this kind of imaginative contemplation. Would Jesus want me to stay with him as he prays on the mountainside? Does he want a shoulder to cry on as he weeps over Jerusalem? Does he need to pour out his feelings, too? What can I do for Jesus in his shame? Does he want me to stay with him in the garden of Gethsemane? One person spent the whole of an eight day retreat staying with Jesus as he endured his passion, even helping him at one point to get up and go on. Can I wipe his face or give him a cup of water? Does he suffer still as he lives with people who are tortured for their beliefs? Would he like to talk about his feelings with me? How does he feel about my presence with him in this kind of contemplation? These are only a few of the questions that might arise in us once we allow ourselves to read the gospels imaginatively with the desire to know Jesus better in order to love him more deeply and to follow him more closely.

Chapter XIII

What Is Jesus Like?

In *The Challenge of Jesus* John Shea says of Jesus that he was a Jew of the first commandment. "For Jesus, the Covenant God is the Lord his God and there are no other gods before him. . . . Every breath Jesus draws tells the story of God. His overriding concern and the organizing center of his personality and activity is He who sent him" (p. 63). It is good to remind ourselves that whatever else we must say of Jesus we must never lose sight of the fact that he was (and is) a human being, a very particular human being, a Jew born in captive Palestine, a believing Jew whose focus was not on himself, but on Yahweh, the one, true God. Given the history, tradition and teaching to which we have been exposed many of us Christians tend to stress the divinity of Jesus and neglect his humanity. Yet the problem set for the early disciples and their followers was not how God could become a human being; rather it was how to make sense of the experience they had of this Jew named Jesus, especially after the resurrection. They experienced the presence of the same Jesus with whom they had walked and eaten in Palestine, and the experience felt like the experience of God himself. We need the help of the Spirit to experience that same mystery, to experience Jesus as a real human being who nonetheless is the Son of God. One way of giving the Spirit the chance to lead us in this direction is to contemplate the gospels with the desire we spoke of in the last chapter, the desire to know him better in order to love him more and to follow him more closely. Another way to translate the same desire is with the question: "What are you like, Jesus?"

I propose to take some passages of Mark's gospel and to point out possible answers to the question just posed. For this purpose I call upon my own experience of contemplating the gospel but also upon my memory of experiences described to me by many people on retreat and in spiritual direction. I do this with some fear and trembling because of the danger that some will take these experiences as normative. Yet I do not know any other means of inviting readers to explore possibilities than by pointing out some ways that Jesus has revealed himself to people. At the same time I must enter the caution: no one else's experience is normative for me or you. Every friendship is unique; what happens between you and me has never happened before in exactly this way because you and I are each unique. Thus our relationship is unique and its uniqueness constitutes our friendship. The same is true of each person's relationship with Jesus; it is not one more instance of "the same old thing." One of the reasons why spiritual direction is so exciting for me is that each person I see has a new story to tell about the relationship with God or Jesus. With this caution let us proceed to look at selected passages in Mark's gospel.

For the moment I pass over the baptism of Jesus, which is his entry onto the stage of the gospel. We shall return to it later. Right after the baptism we read: "After John was put in prison, Jesus went into Galilee, proclaiming the good news of God. 'The time has come,' he said. 'The kingdom of God is near. Repent and believe the good news!' " (1:14–15). We do not often put together the notions of repentance and good news. What does Jesus mean? In a sense the rest of the gospel answers that question. God has come absolutely close in Jesus, and that closeness requires a change of heart and mind about ourselves and about God, and that closeness is good news indeed.

Recently at the end of a liturgy we all sang the song:

> I heard the voice of Jesus say, 'Come unto me and rest;
> lay down, thou weary one, lay down thy head upon my
> breast'.
> I came to Jesus as I was, weary and worn and sad;
> I found in him a resting place, and he has made me glad.
>
> I heard the voice of Jesus say, 'Behold, I freely give
> the living water; thirsty one, stoop down and drink, and
> live'.
> I came to Jesus, and I drank of that life-giving stream;
> my thirst was quenched, my soul revived, and now I live
> in him.
>
> I heard the voice of Jesus say, 'I am this dark world's
> light;
> look unto me, thy morn shall rise, and all thy day be
> bright'.
> I looked to Jesus, and I found in him my star, my sun;
> and in that light of life I'll walk till travelling days are
> done.

I had a hard time singing the song because of my tears of joy as I realized how much Jesus is good news for me. Closeness to him delights me and overwhelms me with gratitude. And I presume that the popularity of the song means that others share the same feelings.

In the next section of the gospel Jesus sees Simon and his brother Andrew and then John and his brother James. To both sets of brothers he simply says, "Come, follow me," and they leave their fishing gear and follow him. Even granted that we may not know in full detail the actual historical call of these first four disciples, still we sense the presence of an enormously attractive personality. What was he like? What is he like for me?

Tales of mythic heroes have always had a strong attraction for human beings. We love to read of (or see now in movies) great leaders who rally people around them to overcome evil. Homer's *Iliad* and *Odyssey*, Vergil's *Aeneid*, the legends of King Arthur and his knights, and many more continue to exert an attraction on us. The attraction to the hero of the Western movie is of the same kind. In recent years the tremendous popularity of J. R. R. Tolkien's trilogy, *The Lord of the Rings*, testifies to the same pull. In his *Spiritual Exercises* Ignatius counts on this primeval pull by having the retreatant reflect on an imaginary king much like King Aragorn in *The Lord of the Rings*. Then, in effect, he says, "Jesus is even better than your dreams." Do we sense some of the excitement of meeting Jesus with such hopes burning in us?

The scenes that follow the call of the first disciples show them something of who Jesus is. He drives out the demon and cures Peter's mother-in-law and many others of illness. What kind of man is this? What does he reveal to us about his hopes, his dreams? When he goes off to pray "very early in the morning, while it was still dark," what is the experience like for him, this Jew of the first commandment? Perhaps we may want to ask him to teach us how to pray, just as later the disciples asked.

What is he like? "A man with leprosy came to him and begged him on his knees, 'If you are willing, you can make me clean.' Filled with compassion, Jesus reached out his hand and touched the man." Touched a leper! Not only risking the disease himself, but also becoming unclean in the eyes of the law. What kind of a man is he, indeed? " 'I am willing,' he said. 'Be clean!' Immediately the leprosy left him and he was cured" (1:40–42). One translation of Jesus' words is: "Of course, I want to." If Jesus is the revelation of God, then here we see God's human reaction to human suffering, just as Jesus' stern rebuke to the evil spirit is God's human reaction to the presence of evil in the world.

Chapter 2 and the beginning of chapter 3 show us the actions that eventually bring Jesus to the cross. He forgives sins, eats and drinks with tax collectors and sinners (and rebukes those who take umbrage at this kind of table fellowship), declares himself lord of the sabbath, and finally heals a man with a shriveled hand on the sabbath—and in a synagogue. "Then the Pharisees went out and began to plot with the Herodians how they might kill Jesus" (3:6). What is he like? How does he seem to you? How do you react when you see him "look around at them in anger, deeply distressed at their stubborn hearts" (3:5)?

"Jesus went up on a mountainside and called to him those he wanted, and they came to him. He appointed twelve—designating them apostles—that they might be with him and that he might send them out to preach and to have authority to drive out demons" (3:13–15). What is he like as he chooses his closest followers? How do you feel as you watch him choosing? Do you want to be chosen? Are you afraid of being passed over? Are you afraid that he might choose you? Notice that the twelve are chosen to do the same things that Jesus has just been doing, preaching the good news and casting out demons. They may know in their bones that they will get the same treatment as Jesus got if they follow him. How does Jesus feel about Judas Iscariot, "who betrayed him"? One thing is sure: when we make poor choices of friends or of those to trust, Jesus can understand us since he did the same thing.

How does Jesus feel when his family thinks that he is crazy and the leaders of his own religion think that he is possessed by a demon? If we have ever been misunderstood or falsely accused, then we have some idea of what he might have felt, but we can also ask him to reveal how he felt and how he handled his feelings. When a bit later he looks around him and says, "Here are my mother and my brothers! Whoever does God's will is my brother and sister and mother," do you feel included in the sweep of his eyes? How do you feel? How does he feel about you as he includes you in the circle? And who else is included in the circle? One person realized as he looked around that the circle included not only many of his friends, but also many people whom he did not know and even people he did not like. What kind of a man is this who includes so many different kinds of people among his family?

Let's move now to the fifth chapter and the healing of the demon-possessed man. As you read the passage, note the savagery of the man and his strength. Imagine how terrified you would be if you were near such a person. Then notice how Jesus approaches him without any protection. Such powerful evil does not seem to frighten him. What kind of man is this? Perhaps we can understand why the townspeople "were afraid . . . and began to plead with Jesus to leave their region" (5:15–17). How do you react when Jesus refuses to let the cured man stay with him?

In the sixth chapter we read about the beheading of John the Baptist. How did Jesus feel when he heard about this sorry deed, this whimsical bit of cruelty that cut off the life of this good man in his prime? Perhaps he does know what it is like when we lose loved ones too early, when life seems so capricious.

In chapter 7 we meet a very strange Jesus in the scene with the Syrophoenician woman (7:24–30). Jesus seems to us cruel and insensitive when this non-Jew asks him to drive out the demon from her daughter. " 'First let the children eat all they want,' he told her, 'for it is not right to take the children's bread and toss it to their dogs.' " No matter how we try to explain these words, they seem to tell us that Jesus was a limited human being who had something to learn from the love and faith of this Gentile woman. In this scene we see in stark outline that Jesus is a Jew whose vision of his mission seems to be limited by his race and religion. In this he is only human. All human beings are limited by their birth, their family, their nationality and culture and religion. But Jesus has the freedom to listen to the riposte of the woman and to change his mind, to learn something. This is one way of contemplating the scene. How does he seem to you?

In the chapters that are bounded by the healing of two blind men, 8:22 and 10:52 we see Jesus becoming more aware of impending doom. Three times he predicts his passion and death; he seems intent on communicating to his disciples what will happen. Three times they are, in effect, blind. After the first prediction Peter denies that any such thing can happen; after the second the apostles argue on the road about which of them is the greatest; after the third James and John come to him and ask to sit at his right hand and his left in the kingdom, thereby angering the other ten. How does Jesus feel as he tries to make them understand what is happening? Does he hope that they will understand and give him some companionship in his plight? How does he feel as he sees the storm clouds gathering? How do you feel toward him?

To end this chapter let us look at the transfiguration (9:2–8) with its obvious reference to the baptism of Jesus in the Jordan (1:9). At the baptism we read: "As Jesus was coming up out of the water, he saw heaven being torn open and the

Spirit descending on him like a dove. And a voice came from heaven: 'You are my Son, whom I love; with you I am well pleased.' " How did Jesus feel as he heard these words, he the Jew of the first commandment? We can ask him to reveal this to us. Now at the transfiguration Jesus has another profound experience of God. At least one can read the scene this way even if some commentators see the scene as a post-resurrection appearance translated to the public life. Jesus has just predicted the passion for the first time; he can sense the hatred and venom beginning to surround him. At this critical juncture he once again hears the words, "This is my Son, whom I love. Listen to him." What a comfort these words must have been to him. After all, it is the leaders of God's religion who are out to kill Jesus. Could he have had doubts about the course he was on? I know people who have cried with joy that Jesus heard such words of warmth and love and reassurance from God in this dark hour. And they have felt that the memory of this experience sustained him in the garden of Gethsemane. How does the scene strike you? What is Jesus like for you?

Chapter XIV

What Does Jesus Value?

In any close friendship the friends share values with one another. Indeed, they gradually take on one another's values, sometimes by osmosis, without even trying to do so. Close friends come to share tastes and values in food, clothing, reading, politics, art, and even friends. As we get to know Jesus better, we begin to notice not only what he is like but also what he values. In this chapter I want to point out some ways of paying attention to Jesus' values.

In the last chapter we noted, with John Shea, that Jesus was a Jew of the first commandment. God is his prime value, beside whom there is no other. " 'Teacher, which is the greatest commandment in the Law?' Jesus replied: 'Love the Lord your God with all your heart and with all your soul and with all your mind. This is the first and greatest commandment' " (Mt 22:36–38). He shows in practice how deep-seated is his own commitment to this commandment.

> On reaching Jerusalem, Jesus entered the temple area and began driving out those who were buying and selling there. He overturned the tables of the money changers and the benches of those selling doves, and would not allow anyone to carry merchandise through the temple courts. And

as he taught them, he said, "Is it not written: 'My house
will be called a house of prayer for all nations'? But you
have made it 'a den of robbers.' " (Mk 11:15–17)

The first commandment is written into his heart and soul.
Jesus values time with his God. He spent forty days in the
desert before his public ministry began. Regularly he seems
to have taken time off to pray. "Very early in the morning,
while it was still dark, Jesus got up, left the house and went
off to a solitary place, where he prayed" (Mk 1:35). After the
feeding of the five thousand "Jesus made his disciples get
into the boat and go on ahead of him to Bethsaida, while he
dismissed the crowd. After leaving them, he went up on a
mountainside to pray" (Mk 6:45–46). He prayed at the transfiguration and in the garden of Gethsamane. And in Luke's
gospel we read: "One day Jesus was praying in a certain
place. When he finished, one of his disciples said to him,
'Lord, teach us to pray, just as John taught his disciples' "
(Lk 11:1). The disciples observed Jesus praying and wanted
to learn from him. The fact that Jesus prayed so much indicates that prayer was a value for him, something he wanted
to do, liked to do, perhaps even needed to do. This fact alone
tells us something about how Jesus experienced God. God
was not someone who terrified him.

And his response to the disciple who asked to teach them
to pray let them and us into his inner life. God is Abba,
Daddy, dear Father. One could just as well say, Mommy,
dear Mother since God has no gender. The point is that Jesus
experiences God, the one and only God, the Creator of the
universe, the Holy, the awesome One, as a tender, warm,
loving parent. Moreover, this God is also our Abba. "When
you pray, say: 'Father, hallowed be your name.' "

Even in his agony in the garden and on the cross Jesus still
calls God Abba. Even in this extremity he still trusts that

God is Abba. "Father, into your hands I commit my spirit" (Lk 23, 46). That is the measure of his trust in the God whom he spent so much time with during his life.

We get another view of how deeply Jesus experienced God as Abba in his anger at the leaders of God's religion because they not only have misunderstood God for themselves, but even more have burdened others with such a false idea of who God is.

> Now then you Pharisees clean the outside of the cup and dish, but inside you are full of greed and wickedness. You foolish people! Did not the one who made the outside make the inside also? But give what is inside the dish to the poor, and everything will be clean for you.
>
> Woe to you Pharisees, because you give God a tenth of your mint, rue and all other kinds of garden herbs, but neglect justice and the love of God. You should have practiced the latter without leaving the former undone. . . .
>
> And you experts in the law, woe to you, because you load people down with burdens they can hardly carry, and you yourselves will not lift one finger to help them. . . .
>
> Woe to you experts in the law, because you have taken away the key to knowledge. You yourselves have not entered, and you have hindered those who were entering. (Lk 11:39–52)

Jesus' anger blazed fiercely at those who kept people from knowing the true nature of God.

Jesus also displayed who God is by his actions. Because he knew God so intimately, he reached out with compassion to touch the leper, to heal the sick, to cure the blind. "Jesus went through all the towns and villages, teaching in their synagogues, preaching the good news of the kingdom and healing every disease and sickness. When he saw the crowds, he had compassion on them, because they were harassed and helpless, like sheep without a shepherd" (Mt 9:35–36). Another time he said:

> I praise you, Father, Lord of heaven and earth, because you have hidden these things from the wise and learned, and revealed them to little children. Yes, Father, for this was your good pleasure.
>
> All things have been committed to me by my Father. No one knows the Son except the Father, and no one knows the Father except the Son and those to whom the Son chooses to reveal him.
>
> Come to me, all you who are weary and burdened, and I will give you rest. Take my yoke upon you and learn from me, for I am gentle and humble in heart, and you will find rest for your souls. For my yoke is easy and my burden is light. (Mt 11:25–30)

And he ate with tax collectors, prostitutes, and other sinners. Why? "It is not the healthy who need a doctor, but the sick. I have not come to call the righteous, but sinners to repentance" (Lk 5:31). In other words, God is Abba even for the outcasts, the pariahs of society and of official religion.

The Sermon on the Mount (Mt 5:1 to 7:29) provides a prime source for learning what Jesus values. We can spend a lifetime pondering and reflecting on these chapters, asking to take on the mind and heart of Jesus. We can also keep contemplating the gospels, desiring to know Jesus, in order to love him more and follow him more closely. To follow him more closely means to live by his values, to be a person of the first commandment, but also to live the second great commandment, "Love your neighbor as yourself" (Mt 22:39). The full meaning of this commandment, and therefore of what Jesus values next in importance to God, is brought home to us in the final judgment scene of Matthew 25:31–46. Let us turn to this great parable to end this chapter.

When the Son of Man comes in his glory, and all the angels with him, he will sit on his throne in heavenly glory. All the nations will be gathered before him, and he will separate the people one from another as a shepherd separates the sheep from the goats. He will put the sheep on his right and the goats on his left.

Then the King will say to those on his right, "Come, you who are blessed by my Father; take your inheritance, the kingdom prepared for you since the creation of the world. For I was hungry and you gave me something to eat, I was thirsty and you gave me something to drink, I was a stranger and you invited me in, I needed clothes and you clothed me, I was sick and you looked after me, I was in prison and you came to visit me."

Then the righteous will answer him, "Lord, when did we see you hungry and feed you, or thirsty and give you something to drink? When did we see you a stranger and invite you in, or needing clothes and clothe you? When did we see you sick or in prison and go to visit you?"

The King will reply, "I tell you the truth, whatever you did for one of the least of these brothers of mine, you did for me."

With whom does Jesus identify? The hungry, the thirsty, the stranger, the naked, the sick, the prisoner, the least of his brothers and sisters. If we love these brothers and sisters, with an effective love that tries to ease their burdens, then we love Jesus. If we do not try to ease their burdens, then, Jesus says, we do not love him. This is indeed a hard saying,

especially in a world such as ours where we are so aware of
the sufferings of so many millions of the brothers and sisters
of Jesus because of the mass media. If at the end we come to
such a hard saying, perhaps we may wish that we had never
asked to know the values of Jesus because the task seems so
impossible. We may all feel that we will be put with the
goats. How can we respond?

First, we need to realize that we are asking to know the
values of Jesus, in order to love him more and follow him
more closely. We cannot change our hearts by our own will
power. If Jesus reveals to us what he values, then he will
also give us the desire to want to share his values, the desire
to be given a heart like his. We are asking for gift, in other
words.

In his autobiography, *The Sacred Journey*, Frederick Buechner recounts an event that sheds light on our perplexity. He
had just signed a contract for his first novel in the offices of
Alfred Knopf. As he left the office, he ran into a former college
classmate who was working as a messenger boy. "I was," says
Buechner, "as I thought, on the brink of fame and fortune. But
instead of feeling any pride or sense of superior accomplish-
ment by the comparison, I remember a great and unheralded
rush of something like sadness, almost like shame." He re-
flects on his luck and his classmate's lack of luck. They part
without saying much of anything to one another. Then
Buechner muses: "All I can say now is that something small
but unforgettable happened inside me as the result of that
chance meeting—some small flickering out of the truth that,
in the long run, there can be no real joy for anybody until
there is joy finally for us all—and I can take no credit for
it. . . . What I felt was something better and truer than I was,
or than I am, and it happened, as perhaps all such things do, as
a gift" (p. 97). What we can do is to contemplate Jesus' life and
values with hope and trust that, like Buechner, we will be

given the gift of a compassionate heart so that we will feel for all our unfortunate brothers and sisters, and not turn our gaze away from their plight. Compassion is the beginning of doing something.

Secondly, we can take heart from the fact that the apostles lived cheek by jowl with Jesus for three years and still did not really know his values. When the Samaritans did not welcome Jesus into their town, James and John asked, " 'Lord, do you want us to call fire down from heaven to destroy them?' But Jesus turned and rebuked them" (Lk 9:54–55). Since it is a gift that we are asking for, we need to be patient with ourselves as we wait for the gift.

At the same time, we try not to turn our gaze away from the hunger and thirst and homelessness and sickness in our midst and on our television screens. We pray to be able to look on our world as it really is with the compassionate eyes of Jesus and to have the heart and gumption to do our bit to ease the burdens, to right the wrongs, to comfort the comfortless. If we continue to contemplate Jesus and to ask to share his values, we can be sure that his grace will not be wanting to us.

Chapter XV

Conclusion

W e can conclude our discussion of a developing intimacy with God and with Jesus by focusing on a question that crops up in most of us when we become friends with someone. Does my friend appreciate my presence and my friendship? I know how delighted I am to know and love Jesus, but how does he feel toward me? Do we give Jesus a chance to tell us what our friendship means to him? Through my own spiritual direction I realized that I was strangely resistant to giving him that chance. Others may note the same defensive resistance in themselves. Let us reflect a bit on the phenomenon.

This resistance may stem from a fear that Jesus is happy that we are happy, but that each of us is just one of the crowd to him. Some people do, I believe, look on Jesus as the great philanthropist who passes out gifts and favors, but neither needs nor is much affected by their friendship. On a retreat recently I began to sense that Jesus was grateful to me for my friendship. Almost immediately I thought of Jesus' words in Luke's gospel: "So you also, when you have done everything you were told to do, should say, 'We are unworthy servants; we have only done our duty' " (Lk 17:10). But then I felt that Jesus said something like this:

"You can think of yourself as an unworthy servant, if you want to, but wouldn't I be an ingrate if I were not grateful to people who have befriended me, worked with me, and suffered with me?" Then I realized that Jesus really is human, and that it is only human to be happy and grateful when you are loved. After all, friendship is mutual.

We may also resist giving Jesus a chance to tell us how much he appreciates our friendship because we run away from that kind of intimacy. We want to be loved and cared for and appreciated, but something in us shies away from an open declaration of love by a friend. At least I can say this of myself. Part of my reluctance to give Jesus a chance to tell me how he feels about me stems from such a dynamic, one that operates in many relationships. I fit rather well the description of a "Two," one of the nine personality types in the Sufi Enneagram: "TWOS avoid recognizing they have *needs. . . .* They pride themselves in being *helpful,* especially to anyone special to them. As regards themselves they do not admit they need others for any help, nor that they have needs which they should attend to themselves" (Maria Beesing, Robert J. Nogosek, and Patrick H. O'Leary, *The Enneagram: A Journey of Self Discovery,* p. 11). Of course, people with this personality type do have needs for appreciation and love; they just have trouble admitting, even to themselves, and asking for what they need. It took me a long time to say outright to Jesus, "Tell me how you feel about me," and then to wait around for an answer.

If we want friendship with Jesus and Jesus wants friendship with us, then we need to give Jesus a chance to express his care and concern for us, just as he gives us a chance to tell him how much we need and appreciate him. When people do give him that chance, he seems to relish the opportunity. Our reluctance to give him the chance may be the last-ditch effort of our ambivalence toward intimacy with God to assert itself. When we become aware of this resistance, we can ask the Lord for the grace to become free enough to surrender our fearful need to save ourselves and prove ourselves worthy of his love. Such a freedom will open the door to an intimacy deeper than we could ever imagine.

Annotated Bibliography

Readers may find the following books helpful:

Barry, William A., *God and You: Prayer as a Personal Relationship.* Mahwah, NJ: Paulist, 1987.

Beesing, Maria, Nogosek, Robert J., and O'Leary, Patrick H., *The Enneagram: A Journey of Self Discovery.* Denville, NJ: Dimension Books, 1984. Very helpfully explains the Sufi Enneagram and relates the personality types to the spiritual life. When used wisely and in moderation, the enneagram has been found helpful by many.

Buechner, Frederick, *The Sacred Journey.* San Francisco: Harper & Row, 1982. An autobiographical memoir whose aim is to show how God has spoken in the ordinary events of the author's life.

Carmody, John, *The Quiet Imperative: Meditations on Justice and Peace Based on Readings from the New Testament.* Nashville, TN: The Upper Room, 1986. Each chapter gives a text to ponder and then a meditation based on the text. Helpful reflections by a man who combines sound scholarship with a passionate concern for God and God's world.

Carmody, John, *Like an Ever-Flowing Stream: Meditations on Justice and Peace Based on Readings from the Old Testament.* Nashville, TN: The Upper Room, 1987. The same format with the Old Testament.

Metz, Barbara and Burchill, John, *The Enneagram and Prayer.* Denville, NJ: Dimension Books, 1987. Presupposes knowledge of the Enneagram from a book like that by Beesing, *et al.* Relates the insights of the Enneagram to prayer.

Moore, Sebastian, *Let This Mind Be in You: The Quest for Identity Through Oedipus to Christ.* San Francisco: Harper &

Row/Seabury), 1985. A dense, but brilliant work by one of the most original spiritual theologians writing today.

Reiser, William E., *Drawn to the Divine: A Spirituality of Revelation.* Notre Dame, IN: Ave Maria Press, 1987. Speaks of the experience of God in our ordinary lives in an engaging, down-to-earth way.

Wright, John H., *A Theology of Christian Prayer.* New York: Pueblo, 1979. A helpful theological guide to understanding prayer in a secular age.